My Words Are Gonna Linger

My Words Are Gonna Linger

The Art of Personal History

Edited by
Paula Stallings Yost
 and Pat McNees

Foreword by
Rick Bragg

Personal History Press

Published by
Personal History Press
43 Beach Avenue
Kennebunk, ME 04043
aph@personalhistorians.org

My Words Are Gonna Linger: The Art of Personal History
Edited and with introductory material by Paula Stallings Yost and Pat McNees
Foreword by Rick Bragg

Library of Congress Control Number: 2008933141

ISBN 978-0-9820134-0-3

First Edition
Printed in the United States of America

Cover design, book design and layout by Marion Johnson
The Memory Works, LLC, Sedona, Arizona

Acknowledgments

Storytelling is both a deeply human impulse and a powerful way to convey one generation's values and memories to those that follow. Understanding our own stories leads to personal growth and self-awareness, and sharing our stories helps build stronger families, friendships, and community. What connects the members of the Association of Personal Historians (APH) is a passion for helping people share and preserve their stories. That passion led to *My Words Are Gonna Linger: The Art of Personal History*, the collection of true stories you hold in your hands.

We owe special thanks to Jeanne Archer, who envisioned this anthology one chilly evening in the warm stacks of the Tattered Cover Book Store, during an APH conference in Denver. With the support of the APH board of directors, Jeanne nurtured this project during her tenure as president (2006-2007). Through the hard work she shared with several dedicated volunteers—Enid Grigg, Catherine Heighway, Stephanie Kadel Taras, Judith Kolva, and Pat McNees, on the original committee—that vision is now reality.

We are also grateful to our members who, along with their students or clients, submitted original pieces for consideration. The responsibility for reviewing and selecting stories fell to Jeanne Archer, Judith Kolva, and Pat McNees. As a member of the second-review team, along with Paula Yost, I appreciate the difficulty of that process, which meant leaving out some very good stories.

Throughout the process, we enjoyed assistance by our APH colleagues. Marty Walton, APH Operations Manager, tracked progress and smoothed efforts along the way. Trena Cleland and Shizue Seigel offered invaluable suggestions on how to organize the collection. Judith Kolva, Debra Moore, Shizue Seigel, and Sharon Waldman provided crucial support as our proofreading team. And Anne Washburn generously volunteered her time and expertise to create the index.

Special thanks go to editor Paula Yost and project manager Pat McNees. Paula's deft and judicious editing allowed each piece to blossom, as did her attention to detail in working with Marion Johnson, the graphic artist who so beautifully designed this book. Pat helped Paula with editing and attending to the many details involved in publication.

To all who volunteered time and expertise to this labor of love, thank you.

PAULA STAHEL
President
Association of Personal Historians

"*There was never yet an uninteresting life.*
Such a thing is an impossibility.
Inside the dullest exterior there is
a drama, a comedy, and a tragedy."

—Mark Twain

Note for table of contents:

If a personal historian is the narrator of the story, his or her name alone appears below the story title. All other entries first list the narrator/storyteller and then, in parentheses, the name of the personal historian who contributed the piece.

Contents

Part One – Why Create A Personal History?

Part Two— Putting the Pieces Together

Part Three – The Many Faces of Personal History

Foreword

Why We Write It Down

People often ask why I built my life as an author on personal stories, family stories, and it always makes me smile. I guess I could try to explain how important it is that we, as a culture, try to preserve the stories that swirl around us all our lives—that, between baby rattles and rattling bones, there exist the true stories of a people, stories just as important as those captured by the captains of industry, government, celebrity, and war.

I guess I should try and argue that the woman with a baby slung on her hip, waiting outside a jail or even on a welfare line, has a story as compelling, as important, as anyone, and that the generations that came before, that brought her to this, are more than just a treadmill of hopelessness. Or, I could argue that a man who teaches at a junior high or sells insurance or Pontiacs for a living has reason to want to dig back into his lineage, to discover—and share—the stories of generations. I could argue that not everyone has the skill or the time or even the lasting will to tell it, but everyone really does have a story.

But I'd rather write about Wild Bill.

I saw Wild Bill for the last time in the backyard of what had been my grandmother's house, a house now painted brown but one we still called "the red house" and will for all our lives, because that is the color it had been when she was alive. When Ava Bundrum died, when I was still a young man, it really ceased to matter what color the old house was.

No one lives in it now, and no one ever will again, because it was her house, and how can anyone ever walk those boards, that tattered linoleum, except her?

But I wander. It was a holiday, the last time I saw my Uncle Bill, her second-oldest child and second son. It was hot so it had to be July Fourth, or Labor Day, and Wild Bill was sitting on a bench in the backyard, not far from the plum trees. He had been ill, and now he sat in the cool shade of the yard—where I used to run barefoot, searching for frogs and chicken snakes—and remembered his momma.

They had been living on a mountain ridge somewhere in the vicinity of Rome, Georgia, and he was just a boy. The little, raggedy house they rented perched on the mountain-side, and it was a green and lovely place most of the time, when the weather was good.

But that day, the one he was remembering, the sky was black and purple and green, and a great storm, a terrible storm, growled and gnawed its way toward them across the treetops. The air filled with the pistol shots of snapping pines, and the treetops whipped and the mighty trunks came crashing down, centuries of life knocked down in a second or two of wind.

And it just came on. They could see it all from their bird's nest of pine boards and ten-penny nails, could see that they had no chance. The children—James, William, Edna, Juanita, Margaret, and maybe Jo, because she might not have been born yet—began to wail. My grandfather, Charlie Bundrum, was an invincible man who had the power to clear the skies, but he was roofing a house in Rome, so they were doomed.

They gathered around Ava and sobbed and screamed, clinging to her skirts, and Ava, who was sharp as a razor, knew that God was cruel, because not only was He about to take her children's lives, He had placed them up high on this ridge to see it coming. The last thing her children felt would be terror.

So she dropped to her knees, to beseech Him. She prayed at first in English but then began to speak in tongues, in old language, language that has passed from this earth. She prayed and prayed and stretched her arms out to heaven, and it must have been quite a show because the children stood around her in awe, because here was something more powerful than storms.

And if the storm had surged in right then and smashed them to bits, Ava would have still won, you see, because her babies would not have died in terror. Puzzlement, yes, but not terror.

But instead, the swirling, terrible storm went left and missed them clean. And it was probably just the nature of storms to do that. All Ava did was stand up, brush off her apron, and look down at her babies.

"Damn," she said. "I thought He had us that time."

Wild Bill is dead. His story, her story, is not.

Amen.

RICK BRAGG
Author of *Ava's Man*
All Over but the Shoutin'
The Prince of Frogtown

Preface

When the Association of Personal Historians was founded in 1995 with approximately fifteen members, maybe one person in a thousand had ever heard of the personal history concept. Today, little over a decade later, the association has grown to almost seven hundred members who have helped thousands worldwide preserve their personal histories. Just in case a few people remain who are not familiar with the concept, we're happy to explain.

What is a personal history? Biography? Autobiography? Memoir? Journal? Scrapbook? Philosophy? Legacy? Family lore? Social history? Business, organizational, or community history? Yes, and so much more. Stories from real life, told in the authentic voices of the storytellers.

Above all, a personal history is a vital link between the past, present, and future—a wisdom-keeper. As the links join together to form chains, they represent the spirit of our families and communities. Thus, we connect to one another and come to understand the purpose of the chain we create by the sharing of our stories.

Perhaps the best way to define personal history is to invite you to join us on this book journey through time, across cultural barriers and socioeconomic lines, through political and social upheavals, even touching on romance. Through the power of stories gathered by our personal historians, you'll tour nineteenth-century Japan, attend an arranged wedding in India in 1925, visit war zones, witness peace demonstrations, dog-sled across the Alaskan tundra, hear a dying mother's last words to her young children, empathize with immigrants escaping political and economic oppression, learn a few secrets behind one of the most noted research facilities in the world...

These are not the literary stories found in *Atlantic Monthly* or the *Yale Review*. They're stories from real people about real life, often told to or written for an audience (usually family) that knows the storyteller. In the end, though, these stories resonate with others because there's something universal about them.

For this anthology, we asked APH members to submit stories they had crafted for or with a particular narrator (storyteller), excerpts from oral histories, stories written by workshop students, or tales from their own lives. We received one hundred thirty-seven entries. Two dedicated selection teams were tasked with choosing the forty-nine stories included within these pages. How we wish there had been enough space for all those great stories.

Authorship is an unusual issue with personal histories. You'll notice in the table of contents that some stories have only one author—the personal historian writing about an event in his or her own life. Others credit first the narrator/author and then, in parentheses, the personal historian who contributed the piece. Occasionally, a third person may be involved if a personal historian's life-writing student has interviewed a narrator and written the story. For each selection, the contributing personal historian has provided a brief explanation as to his or her involvement and, where appropriate, a bit of the author/narrator's background. In most cases, however, the narrator or storyteller is the owner/author of the story or commentary.

To help readers better understand the personal history concept, we have presented the stories in three sections. *Why Create a Personal History*, Part 1, explores a few of the reasons behind our need to share our stories. Often, they are a gift of celebration, a tribute or a memorial. Sometimes we create them out of curiosity about our ancestry or as an extension of genealogy (fleshing out the family tree), sometimes as a journalistic article, or even as part of an oral history project. Organizations also are discovering the power of compelling narrative to memorably convey their missions and strengths. No matter the motivation, our stories become part of a process of life review that goes on all our lives but is particularly important as we age. Ultimately, personal history is a form of tribal communication, a way of reaching out to someone in the distant future to say, "We were here."

Part 2, *Putting the Pieces Together*, demonstrates a few different ways to approach a personal history. Our intent is to help others find the approach that is right for them, whether it's serious reflection, lighthearted storytelling, or something else. If you're interested in collecting your parents' life stories, for instance, you could encourage them to tell their stories to you or to another family member. But if time, distance, or uncertainty is a barrier to writing or recording the story, Mom and Dad might enjoy talking about their lives during a relaxed, conversational interview with a professional personal historian.

Personal historians tend to be excellent listeners who also can simplify and organize the transcription and editing process, and help you select an appropriate package or style.

Our emphasis is on the stories to be told, the people and events remembered. By listening closely, trying to connect the dots, and identifying the patterns in people's lives we sometimes clarify what previously was only a murky or distant memory.

The Many Faces of Personal History, Part 3, suggests a variety of possibilities. There is no right or wrong choice. Some personal historians specialize in video tributes or memorials, while some prefer oral histories (preserving the transcript and voice). More than words, audio histories preserve laughter, song, inflection in voices that will live on. Some clients want an audio-visual product (voice plus still photos or moving pictures) because it can capture voice, body language, and facial expressions. Audio-visual products are especially effective for sharing with a group. Personal historians often are called upon to create videos to celebrate an engagement, a wedding, an anniversary, a birth, a graduation, a retirement, and more.

But many of us love the printed page and place our greatest trust in a book, well printed and bound, knowing it can easily be handed down through the generations and fearing that the latest digital technology could become obsolete almost before we get used to it. A narrative memoir in print typically is enriched with reflections on life's lessons and enlivened by photos with captions. Directly or indirectly, personal histories often also strive to convert experience into wisdom.

Personal histories have been created throughout the ages in all the formats listed within these pages and countless others. Prehistoric petroglyphs etched on canyon walls;

traditions and lore passed down by tribal elders through the generations; grandmothers sharing childhood memories with grandbabies on front-porch swings; artists and technicians creating everything from hand-sewn story quilts to audio voice quilts via the Internet to virtual books online. And we're just getting started …

To paraphrase Willard Watson, the narrator whose words provided this anthology's title, our goal is to make sure your words are gonna linger.

PAULA STALLINGS YOST
PAT MCNEES

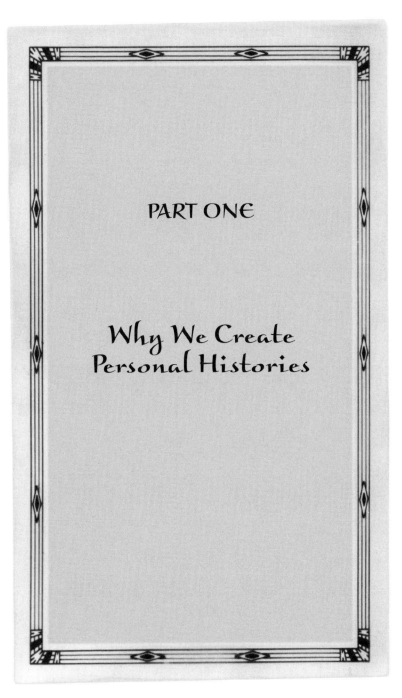

PART ONE

Why We Create
Personal Histories

Introduction

The pieces gathered in this section illustrate a few of the many reasons we create personal histories. To celebrate her parents' fiftieth anniversary, for example, Paula Stahel ("A Gift in Return") wanted to give them a one-of-a-kind gift. She invited two hundred of their friends and relatives to send photos and written memories of her parents' lives, which she then assembled into a "This Is Your Life" album and presented to them at a surprise anniversary party. Similarly, Judith Kolva was asked to create a joint personal history for a couple celebrating their love for each other after sixty years together.

A personal history also can be a memorial, as in Paula Yost's "Daffodil Fields"—a fond remembrance of the larger-than-life grandmother who raised her.

Sometimes we tell our stories as a legacy for future generations, offering them a window into worlds they otherwise would never know. Nellie Nakamura's son asked Shizue Seigel to record Nellie's oral history, combine it with family photos and some historical Japanese background, and create a book. Flavia Fernandes's daughter commissioned a personal history of her mother as a gift in honor of Flavia's eightieth birthday, including the excerpt herein that describes the arranged marriage of Flavia's parents in Mangalore, India, in 1925. Susan Rothenberg found Johnny Wilson's story so compelling that she offered to create an oral history for his family. Jeanne Archer collected her father's stories about his adventures on a submarine during World War II after realizing that even her teenage daughter found them interesting.

Memories sometimes are recorded as a tribute to courage, kindness, and generosity of spirit. "The Hannan Family" vividly conveys how compassion and a strong sense of justice led some "ordinary heroes" to take action when so many others failed even to be aware of the injustices inflicted on Japanese-Americans during their internment after the Japanese government's attack on Pearl Harbor. "Beacons of Light in a Dark Time" is Quentin Brown's tribute to two people—a kind German nurse and a wartime buddy—who helped him survive a grim period as a seriously wounded prisoner of war captured by the Nazis.

Many of the stories we collect record an ordinary person's experience of an extraordinary personage or historical event, especially once we realize the storyteller won't always be around. George McCoy was eighty-three when he told Gillian Hewitt what life was really like in the trenches of World War II. When Cynthia McLean's mother, Mary, fell off her horse at the age of seventy-eight, Cynthia began recording and transcribing the stories of Mary's life to divert her from the pain and outrage of broken bones, including the story about her experiences as a wartime volunteer with General George S. Patton in Europe.

Sometimes we tell stories both to create a sense of community and to set the record straight. Commissioned by the National Institutes of Health to write a fiftieth anniversary history of the NIH Clinical Center, Pat McNees interviewed dozens of people to find such stories as the one published herein about early NIH experiments in cancer chemotherapy. She found the human story that would help convey the courage of the patients and their families, the informed creativity and perseverance of the researchers, and the caring nature of the medical staff.

Creating a personal history also can be a voyage of self-discovery—a way to make sense of our lives and the past while reflecting on lessons learned. As an exercise in life-story writing, Bea Epstein created a verbal portrait of her parents and bravely explored the shadow side of their marriage, acknowledging as an adult the reality she couldn't understand, or change, as a child. Sandra Choukroun wrote the story of her search for a book read in childhood that held a strange grip on her—the rediscovery of which helped her arrive at a deeper understanding of her childhood.

Personal histories with an emphasis on moral values and lessons learned are sometimes presented in the form of an ethical will—a centuries-old Jewish tradition for conveying one's values, hopes, regrets, apologies, and more to family, friends, and community. Ethical wills may be shared while the authors are still alive or may be read aloud to friends and family after they have died. Bettina Brickell created hers shortly before her death at twenty-nine. Ray Quinn wrote his as an exercise for a workshop.

We tell our stories because we don't want to be forgotten. We want to feel we have made a difference. But why do some of us get involved in helping others tell their stories? To a large extent, we do so simply because we find the process and the stories fascinating. We hope you will agree as you read the stories that follow.

The eldest of five generations in his family, Johnnie Wilson Jr. was born in Louisiana near the beginning of the twentieth century. He lived on his father's farm as a small boy, until the tragic death of his parents forced him to leave and move in with his grandparents. I heard about Mr. Wilson from one of his grandsons, was fascinated by his story, and offered to create an oral history for him. Mr. Wilson and I worked together for almost two years, until his death at age ninety-five, recording his life story and producing a book, Johnnie Wilson Jr.: To Be a Man. *Initially, the book was intended solely for his family, but his story was so compelling that it was later released commercially.*

—Susan Gluck Rothenberg

Like My Daddy Started Me

Johnnie Wilson Jr., Narrator

Even though I was young when my daddy died, I learned how to do things by my daddy. I went everywhere he went. I was right there with him. I learned so much from following him, just to see what all he do and how he make a living. He worked hard, and whatever he did, he did good. That's what counts. Just thinking about what he did kept me going when things were tough. How my daddy raised me stayed with me.

Johnnie Wilson Sr. purchased a farm in 1910, evicting the previous owner, a white man.

Daddy was a big farmer. He had six people working for him, and he made a good farm every year. They raised everything they needed on the farm. Daddy raised sugar cane and made his own syrup. He also raised cotton, corn, sweet potatoes, and popcorn. We had plenty of everything—chickens, hogs, guineas, and ducks. He was doing fine there. Never had to borrow nothing from nobody.

After we moved to the farm, I started working out in the fields with my daddy, just to be with him. I learned how to plow and help him in the fields. Everywhere he went, I was right there with him, doing anything he needed that I could do. I just wanted to help him. I learned how to do everything from my daddy.

There weren't many black men who owned farms where we were. Most worked for white men. Black men owning farms in Louisiana didn't have long lives. They didn't want us to have nothing. It was just so pitiful.

Four years after moving to the farm, Johnnie's parents and several siblings died, from poison in the cistern, he believed. Johnnie went to live with his grandparents, whom he had never met.

My Uncle Coleman would sometimes send Grandpa a package from Houston, and I'd go to the post office to get it. I was a big boy then—thirteen, something like that. But I couldn't sign my name because I ain't never been to school. I signed with an "X." One time, a white man standing there said, "Look at him. As big as he is, he can't sign his own name." He kept looking at me as I walked out of the post office. It hurt me so bad I went to crying once I got outside.

On the side of the road, near where I lived, was an old abandoned Caterpillar machine. I would go by the machine a lot. I knew the name of the machine. Every time I would go by the machine, I would spell that name, Caterpillar, and learned the letters. I could spell caterpillar before I could spell rat or cat. I started to write with a stick, just marking on the ground. That's how I got started learning to read and write.

I figured out words anyway I could. Once I saw a boy, about eight or nine years old, in front of a store window with a sign in it. I asked him, "Do you know what that is?"

He said, "Soda water." He knew how to read the words, but I didn't. Now, he didn't know that I didn't know what it was. And so I learned two new words. That's just how I kept learning. Every way I could, I figured out new words. I don't have education, but I can read and write.

When Johnnie was eighteen, he left his grandparents' home to work on a nearby farm, where he met his wife, Clara, and began his own family.

I needed more money for my family. I was always doing something to improve. I left Emil's farm in 1928 or so and went to work at a sawmill. My job was stacking up lumber. That's where you made the money, stacking lumber. I made about forty some dollars a week.

Back then, Clara and I were always able to live pretty good, even though money was tight. We grew whatever we needed. We only went to the store to get stuff like shortening or meal or flour, something like that. We raised most everything we ate—onions, mustard, cabbage, and sweet potatoes, too. In the summer, we had delicious watermelon. Our garden always made life easier, especially when things got tough. That garden meant a whole lot.

We survived all right because I was able to catch fish and make a garden. I take care of business. That's something I learned from my father. He never had to borrow nothing from nobody. I grow up just in his footsteps. Never had to borrow.

Johnnie decided to leave Louisiana after his area was hit hard by the Depression. His brother-in-law helped him find a job in construction.

I thought about my brother Coleman and Clara's brother Clarence Reed in Galveston, Texas, and in 1934, I finally decided to go join them.

I did a lot of different jobs at Hayden [Construction]. I worked hard to make a living. I was just a man; I had to be a man. I had Clara and [our daughter] Willie Mae to take care of. After I was there for a while, I learned how to

Johnnie in 1939

operate the chair rig by myself. I used to help the rig operator when he went for his twelve o'clock break. I would cut the steam on the rig for him. Then as soon as he go to eat, I turned the steam back on. I fooled with the rig and learned how to operate it just like he did. He would never have showed me how to do it. If he'd known I was fooling with the rig, he'd have died.

One day, I was practicing on the rig. Tucker, my boss, came around and saw the boom moving. When I saw him, I stopped. I come back down there quickly and fooled around down on the ground.

He came over and said, "Get your black behind right on back up that rig."

I went back up, and Tucker watched me operate the rig with no problem. I could swing the rig around, swoop it down, and stop it on a dime. Then swing it back up and start again. I could operate the rig just like that white man did. Same thing. I knew everything by watching him. If anything go wrong, I knew how to fix it just like he did.

The boss-man told me I had a new job, and he gave me a little bit more money. They sent the white man to work at Port Arthur, Texas, one of the other places Hayden had a business. I stayed working where I was. Everybody came and looked to see a black man operating the rig. I let them know I was just as good as the white operator was.

In the 1940s, Johnnie went to work on the Galveston waterfront and earned his union card. He then moved to San Francisco, where he worked as a longshoreman until he retired. He never stopped trying to learn.

I want my children and all of my grandchildren to know that the main thing is knowing how to treat people like you want to be treated. If you got a little more than that person, you don't think that you is better than that person, 'cause you are not.

I ain't nothing but a kid when I went with my daddy to the bank, but listening to them talk, I'm learning from what they say and how they say it. As I grow up, it stays with me: I know how to treat people. From that day to this day, I'm the same way. I get along with everybody. No one but my father taught me anything. I growed up just like my daddy started me.

Johnnie Wilson Jr. at his ninety-fifth birthday party in 2002

For Nellie Nakamura's hundredth birthday, her son David asked me to record her oral history and combine it with historical background information and family photos to create a book. We wanted to preserve the unique flavor of Nellie's speech while providing a sense of how Japanese and Japanese-American history and customs affected Nellie and her family.

—Shizue Seigel

A Trunk of Dreams

Nellie Nakamura with Shizue Seigel

When you're young, you're interested in your own life. It's only after it's too late that you realize, "Gee, I wish I had asked my mother more things." Besides, my mother was kind of close-mouthed. She never volunteered anything; I had to ask. If she didn't want to talk about it, she wouldn't lie; she'd just answer in monosyllables—yes or no. That's the Japanese way. You never say no directly, but you have ways of letting people know.

The only reason I know about Mama's travels is that she had a trunk with stickers of Ceylon, Washington, D.C., London, and Paris. It was a trunk of dreams. When I was little, we were poor farm workers. I'd look at that trunk and think, "Mama could do all this…" I had fantasies about all the travels she was able to make. She had little souvenir spoons from Venice and Paris, and pamphlets from different countries. She had a book that showed beautiful pictures of strange-looking boats. All these things were in the trunk.

My mother, Rui, was born in Japan in 1868. That was the year of the Meiji Restoration, when feudalism was overthrown. She remembered her father cutting off his samurai topknot. I think her family had a hard time adjusting. Those were not happy times.

In 1868, political power was invested in Emperor Meiji, ending 250 years of political and economic stability under the Tokugawa shoguns. With the end of feudalism, clan retainers became masterless—their stipends cut off and lands confiscated. As Japan emerged from its long isolation, some ventured abroad to create new lives for themselves. Perhaps because of the social upheaval of the era, Rui grew up with remarkable freedom, which fostered an independent and adventurous spirit.

Rui Suzuki (second from left) posing for a souvenir photo with friends of Nellie Hill, circa 1897

When Mama was growing up, nobody paid much attention to what she did. While her sister was in the house learning how to cook and clean, Mama sneaked out. She did pretty much what she wanted, like swimming and climbing trees.

By her bedside, Nellie keeps a portrait of her mother shot in 1915. Rui's naturally curly hair is pulled back. Her delicately worked Edwardian blouse contrasts strikingly with her penetrating gaze and determined expression. She looks as independent as an American suffragette.

The picture shows the way she was. She had that expression, like she could see right through you. She was not ever aggressive or pushy, but she didn't let anybody push her around.

My mother never told me, but I sort of figured it out. I think she was promised to someone as a child, and when the time came, she married him, even though she didn't want to. After she had the baby, she just took off. She left the baby because in Japan, that baby belonged to the father's house, especially if there were no other sons in the family.

Rui Suzuki

Upper-class families viewed marriage as a means of advancing wealth or social standing. Liaisons were initiated by the parents through a go-between. Neither the prospective bride nor groom was given much say in the matter. Once married, a woman joined her husband's extended household and rendered absolute obedience to her husband and her parents-in-law. In many cases, she was treated as little more than a servant. Divorce was an inconceivable disgrace. That Rui was willing to step outside the accepted mold is a testament to her strength of character.

Rui Suzuki in Japan, circa 1900

After she left her marriage, my mother went to Osaka. Running away, and doing for herself, made her self-sufficient. She never went to school to learn English. She just took it up! She was a quick person, very quick to learn things. She was working as a salesperson for a fabric store when she met this American woman—a wealthy, single woman. And my mother's life took off from then. *[laughs]*

Life during the Meiji Restoration was both difficult and intoxicating, as new ideas supplanted old ways. Western ways captured the imagination of young and old alike. The Meiji government believed that in order for Japan to maintain its independence and stave off colonization by Western powers, it was imperative for the educated classes to learn and adopt Western ways, particularly in commerce, science, and the military.

Rui must have been exposed to many ideas that caused her to question the role of women in Japanese society. Sometime in the mid-1890s, when Rui would have been in her twenties, she met Nellie Hill, a wealthy traveler from America. Nellie Hill was one of the thousands of upper and middle-class women who broke out of their traditional roles as housewives and society matrons to travel abroad during the late nineteenth century. These "wayward women" were sparked by a handful of colorful and adventurous role models like journalist Nellie Bly (1862-

1922), a champion of women's rights who circled the globe in seventy-two days, and Isabella Bird (1832-1904), whose book, Unbeaten Tracks in Japan *(1880), may have piqued Miss Hill's curiosity about the Land of the Rising Sun.*

It was a lucky day for both of them when Nellie Hill met my mother. Miss Hill was a wealthy private citizen from Groton, Massachusetts, who came by herself to Japan. She liked it so well she went back home and came another time. My mother could speak a little English, so Miss Hill latched on to her. She probably said, "Would you like to be my companion and travel with me?" Mama was willing because she didn't like her life in Japan anyhow. I guess she jumped at the chance.

Nellie Hill's parents were very strict. When Miss Hill went to college and met a man, the only man that she ever fell in love with, her parents wouldn't let her marry him because he was Catholic. She told her parents, "If you're not going to let me marry the man I love, I'm never going to get married. I'm not going to stay around here. I'm just going to go wherever I want to." So she just took off and started going to different countries. They traveled all around Japan and went to China, Ceylon, Italy, France, and England.

Miss Hill was not quite ten years older than my mother. But I guess you could say they were like kindred souls. Even though they were from opposite sides of the world, they both stepped outside the usual roles for women in those days. They were independent and interested in new things; they didn't just do what was expected of them. Miss Hill opened up a whole new world for Mama.

Rui's chance meeting with a wealthy stranger transformed her from a struggling social outcast into a valued traveling companion. The very qualities that had propelled her outside the norms of conventional Japanese society—her irrepressibly adventuresome spirit and her love of learning—became her ticket to a vast and interesting new world.

Rui's facility with the English language and familiarity with Western ways must have delighted Nellie Hill. During the late 1800s, many Westerners, particularly missionaries, traveled in Japan. However, few were lucky enough to find individuals, let alone women, who spoke English and were free to accompany them and help them navigate bureaucratic and cultural stumbling blocks. Miss Hill's appreciation and generosity would open worlds of opportunity not only to Rui but, later, to her children and grandchildren.

Miss Hill was a spinster, but from a prestigious family. She had my mother come and stay with her for a year in the United States. One of her uncles was a congressman in Washington, D.C. When Miss Hill took Mama to see the U.S. Congress in session, she told her to wear a formal kimono. I guess they were an unusual sight in the spectators' gallery—a tall, blond woman in a long Edwardian dress accompanied by a tiny Japanese woman in exotic clothing. That night, the uncle had Miss Hill over for dinner and told her, "Your friend is welcome to visit Congress again, but next time, dress her in Western clothes. You caused too much of a commotion today."

Miss Hill sent my mother to sewing school in Boston for a year. I don't know what happened after that, but I think her family said, "Nellie, you'd better get rid of her. She's…You know…"

We don't really know why Rui returned to Japan. Was New England society so horrified by a friendship that transcended class and race? Were employment opportunities in Boston closed to her? Was she simply homesick? We'll never know. We can guess, however, that the kindhearted Nellie Hill was reluctant to simply abandon her protégé without prospects.

Miss Hill returned with Rui to Japan and helped her establish a small business in Yokohama. Shortly before leaving Japan for the last time, she introduced Rui to Matsunosuke Sumiye, who became Rui's second husband and Nellie Nakamura's father.

Rui (far left) in front of Mikawa-ya, the fabric store she opened in Yokohama with the help of Nellie Hill

Creating a memorable gift for my parents'
fiftieth wedding anniversary led to unexpected
discoveries of my own and resulted in this essay,
which was published in a shorter version in the
St. Petersburg Times *in February 1999.*
—*Paula Stahel*

A Gift in Return

Paula Stahel

"Well... I guess I'll just put my dress back in mothballs."

The pain in Mom's voice, reverberating across 1,250 phone miles, was not a guilt-inducing ploy. And I was the cause. I'd hurt my parents plenty of times before, Lord knows, but this time was intentional.

"I'm sorry. There's just no way I can fly in on Friday," I lied.

Friday would be my parents' fiftieth anniversary. In my mind's eye, I could see the sea-foam green, tea-length linen dress with cutwork embroidery. It still fit her slender form as perfectly as when she'd been married in it.

"When can you make it? We'll ask Gevan and Deni to take us out to dinner then."

Fat chance, I thought. My brother and sister-in-law were in cahoots with me on this.

I begged God to remember I wasn't really lying. I couldn't arrive Friday because my plane would land in Kalamazoo on Tuesday. My sister-in-law and I needed time to finish plans for Friday's dinner and Saturday's surprise bash. Plus, I still hadn't finished the memory book I'd begun months earlier.

For nearly a year, Gevan, Deni, and I had pondered how to mark this milestone. Every idea we came up with eventually fizzled. Finally, it dawned on us that what was important to our parents were the people who'd filled their lives. What was important to those people were the memories our folks had created with them. Since hiring Ralph Edwards for a private version of his 1950s television show, *This Is Your Life*, was beyond our budget, we decided I would create a book chronicling their life together

For weeks, I lay awake at night trying to recall names of grown-ups from my childhood. Gevan and I burned the phone lines, putting names to faces that surfaced in our minds. I searched for addresses through the Internet, enlarging the list of people to contact. That winter, when my parents came from their Arizona home to visit me in Florida, I managed to get my hands on Mom's address book without her knowledge. I set out on a writing campaign. Within a matter of weeks, I'd sent nearly two hundred letters explaining what we were up to. Friends and family were asked to send photos and letters of remembrance about times shared with my folks.

What I remembered most about my parents' lives was struggle—probably the normal struggle of life, but uniquely their own. Building various homes and a popular resort in Michigan's Upper Peninsula. Establishing Dad's business. Their seemingly constant struggle with each other, with my brothers and me. Gevan and I still struggle with parental expectations—the unending rite of any "child's" passage.

Rites of passage continued for Mom and Dad. They'd buried their parents. Married off three children. Become grandparents and great-grands. Seen two of us through divorces and remarriage. And buried their youngest, my brother Mike, within a year of his own parenthood.

Growing up, I never saw my parents in Ward and June Cleaver of *Leave It to Beaver*. To me, they were the Ricardos of *I Love Lucy*. My mother, Mabeline, wasn't red-haired or a comedienne, but she was beautiful and, in her own way, could be ditzy. Like Lucy, she was unable to sit still. Darkly handsome like Ricky, Dad had an accent too, although it was Czech, not Cuban. He wasn't a famous musician, but a master woodworker whose craft was art that brought him local fame. Still, the arguments between the live-wire American wife and the Old World husband were a lot alike.

Later, I saw my parents in different fictional characters. Like Marie Barone on *Everybody Loves Raymond*, Mom can dispense advice freely. Like *Lake Wobegon's* Florian Krebsbach, Dad's ability to tune Mom out drives her to distraction. Like the Barones and the Krebsbachs, my parents snip at each other in their own vernacular. Transcending ethnicity, it's the universal language of longevity, endurance.

Yet these were not the people reflected in the letters and photos that flooded in for the memory book. And in creating this gift for them, I received one, too.

I read of times forgotten or unknown in the natural parent/child struggle. A cousin wrote of my father's patience in teaching him to use a hammer, when patience wasn't something my brothers and I experienced. An aunt wrote that after my birth, Dad refinished a grand piano to earn extra money. With no one to help move it, he crawled underneath and inched it across the floor on his back. Contagious enthusiasm was the theme when it came to Mom. A woman told about the night in Paris when, after the subway closed, Mom convinced everybody in Dad's long-retired Airborne group to jump the turnstiles. The stories went on and on.

After my telephone lie to Mom, my parents asked Gevan to postpone their anniversary dinner. He refused to cancel the reservations and insisted that Mom was to wear her wedding dress. During the week before the event, I stayed hidden in his basement, working madly to compile the memory book pages in an album my artistic sister-in-law had covered in handmade paper. Every time the front door opened upstairs, I feared our folks were dropping by. When Deni and I ran errands, I worried I'd be recognized by someone who knew Mom or Dad.

But on Friday, our secret was still safe. Gevan and Deni went to fetch our folks while I headed to the restaurant. When they arrived, Mom and Dad were shocked to see me with their original wedding party—my dad's only sibling, his brother, who had been his best man, and mom's best friend from high school, who had been her only attendant. Rounding out the group were their spouses and Deni's parents.

When Dad saw the group, he grabbed a handkerchief to swab his eyes. Mom fell against a wall for support. After recovering, she scowled and then laughed. "You kids! I could shoot you!"

Dad said, "This is the best gift you could have given us."

It wasn't. Not yet. Over dinner, Gevan casually suggested, as if he'd just thought of it, that we hold a family cookout the next afternoon.

By noon Saturday, nearly one hundred guests from across the U. S. and Canada had gathered at my brother's home. When Mom arrived, she was startled when a close friend opened the door. Mom's knees again buckled as she saw the crowd. My father swayed woozily, surrounded by relatives and long-unseen buddies from World War II and his work years. As yet another couple arrived, Mom covered her face with her hands. "Who else?" she asked through tears. "Who else?"

Later, in an unusual display of tenderness, Mom and Dad held hands while a quartet sang. Then I presented the memory book. Nearly four hundred pages carried scores of letters and decades of photographs attesting to the love and friendship they'd given away and earned in return.

Our parents were speechless.

Martin and Mabeline Stahel celebrating their fiftieth anniversary with a surprise book of memories from family and friends

But not for long. They're still the Barones, the Krebsbachs, after all. I later learned that my father, the morning after the anniversary celebration, had angrily insisted, "No one, not even the queen of England, is important enough to deserve this!"

"Martin," my mother snapped, "just shut up and say thank you."

For weeks, Mom carried that book everywhere, clasped tightly against her chest. Dad wouldn't open it. Eventually, in private, he did. He told me he could read only a couple pages at a time before emotion overcame him.

Now, as my parents approach their sixtieth anniversary, the memory book sits in their living room. The pages' edges are a bit worn, though I don't see it as wear. It's a patina of love.

I have been privileged to help create a joint personal history for Paul and Jean McGiness at the request of their daughter Linda Radon and granddaughter Jamie Hardesty. The project became a celebration of their lives and their love for each other after sixty years together. The following excerpt from their book, For Our Family: A Memoir of Love, *describes a bit of Paul's humble but happy childhood.*

—Judith Kolva

We Got By

Paul McGiness, Narrator

My family was poor, but that's just the way it was. Because we accepted our circumstances, we got by. From the time we were little kids, my brothers, sisters, and I knew we had to roll up our sleeves and go to work. We were expected to contribute to the common pot. My family worked hard and scraped along, but we were still poor. Every penny we made went into the family pot and was used for food and clothes. Taking money out of the pot was the only way we managed to get by. *Humble* is the word that best described us.

I was born in a farmhouse on October 18, 1919, in Forest Township, Missaukee County, Michigan. I weighed ten pounds, which by all standards made me a big baby. My mother said there was nothing remarkable about my birth. By the time I came along, I guess she was used to having babies. I was the seventh of her nine children, spanning seventeen years: Kathleen, Ida Mae, Doris, Madge, Charlie, James, Paul, Bernice, and Jack. We looked like stairsteps.

Our mother never let us forget that Charlie was special because he was born on November 11, 1918, Armistice Day—the day World War I ended. The treaty was signed at 5:00 a.m, and the fighting stopped in the eleventh hour of the eleventh day of the eleventh month. In celebration, people danced in the streets and drank champagne. *"The war to end all wars"* was over. Church bells rang in hope that the world would never again experience such atrocities. Mother insisted the bells chimed in honor of Charlie's birthday. We knew better, but never got tired of hearing the story.

My parents named me Paul DeWitt McGiness. *DeWitt* is after my dad. Mother said they named me Paul so I wouldn't have any nicknames, but somehow I had more nicknames than all the other kids put together. My brothers and sisters called me *Paudie,* and if that wasn't enough, they also called me *Punk.* When I was in high school and played football, I was kind of squirmy, so my teammates dubbed me *Squirrel.* My mother could never figure it out. She just rolled her eyes and laughed.

My family was a good family. We lived day to day, doing our best to eat three square meals and have a home where we were safe and didn't have to worry. It's not unusual for that many kids to have their little battles, but we got along pretty well for the most part. My name was hollered out quite a few times, so I guess I got into more mischief than the rest of them. I wasn't bad, just impish. I loved to play tricks on my brothers and sisters.

That Charlie was the ornery one. He'd boss us. Then we'd get into scrapes. When our mother wasn't home, Charlie locked me in the closet. It's his fault that I'm afraid of the dark to this day. Directly before I went into the service, I sold my car. When I asked Charlie if I could borrow his, he yelled, "Are you crazy? Absolutely not!"

I guess he got to thinking about how mean he was because a year or so later I got a letter from him, saying, "I know I was kind of ornery to you guys. If I ever see you again, I'm gonna make up for it." And he did. Later in life, anything I wanted from Charlie, I got. Deep down, he was a good guy, just ornery.

I grew up during the Great Depression. Some people had jobs, but most didn't. We'd pick up whatever work we could—a little money here and a little money there. It all helped fill the common pot. There wasn't any welfare like there is now. Today, if you're out of a job, the government has to pay. But back then? No way. In Detroit, mobs of people scrounged the dirty markets for spoiled food. When you're really hungry, you'll do anything. There's no doubt about it, we lived through real bad times.

Even though Kellogg's Bran Flakes cost only ten cents a box, chuck roast ten cents a pound, eggs fifteen cents a dozen, and bacon nineteen cents a pound, people didn't have money to buy these staples. The stock market went upside down, banks closed, and factory doors were nailed shut. The most popular song of the day was "Brother, Can You Spare a Dime?" It was more than a just a song; we lived the words. Life sure wasn't rosy. As a matter of fact, it was pretty doggone bleak. People were down and out. President Hoover claimed good times were just around the corner, but that was hard to believe. It was the Dark Ages all over again. Folks stood in bread lines and got an occasional bite to eat at soup kitchens. Hobos rode the trains, and bandits raided the highways. With unemployment at 25 percent, men who could no longer take care of their families pulled the trigger. Suicide was at an all-time high.

It got so bad that some folks ignored their pride and accepted government handouts. We'd see people lugging cardboard cartons and bulging bags of what everybody knew was government surplus food. You couldn't mistake the huge cans of grapefruit juice, paper sacks of cornmeal, and cellophane bags of rice and prunes. Being on relief was shameful. People who accepted government handouts were scorned, but I guess they had to decide between being embarrassed and feeding their families.

Nothing was handed to us; we had to work for everything. I think people who live high on the hog today wouldn't be so far in debt if they lived like they should, within their means. That's what we did back when I was a kid. We didn't have any place to turn; we didn't have credit cards. We lived on what we earned and held our heads high because we weren't in debt to anybody. People today want everything, and they want it right now. You can't do that. You gotta pay for things. You gotta have a plan.

One day, when I finished doing some chores for an old farmer he called me down to his shed and showed me a bicycle. I opened my eyes wide and said, "Gee, you got a bicycle."

He pulled a ratty handkerchief out of his back pocket, wiped the sweat off his forehead, and replied, "Yep! If you want it, I'll sell it to you for six bucks."

I was so happy I ran all the way home and spilled the good news to my mother. Without looking at me, and continuing to knead her bread, she said, "Paul, we don't have the money." I couldn't have the bicycle. I felt so sad, but I never said a word. That's just the way life was.

Lake City is well known for its potato crop. My brothers and sisters and I learned real young that potatoes were our staple. As long as we had potatoes, we'd never be hungry. Come fall, the kids in the county took a potato vacation from school. For a couple of weeks, the schools closed, and the kids picked potatoes in the farmers' fields. Let me tell you, potato-picking is dirty work, but we didn't complain. We knew Mother would use the money we earned picking potatoes to buy potatoes for us to eat. One year, believe it or not, she put a hundred bushels of potatoes in our cellar. That's a lot of potatoes, but they were my mother's insurance policy. She'd go down the creaky cellar steps, look at those potatoes, and feel safe. She knew her kids would survive the long, cold winter.

After our chores each day, we came in for supper, which was almost always potatoes and gravy. The gravy was Michigan paste. Mother spooned flour into a frying pan and scorched it, then she stirred in some water, and that was our gravy. Along with the potatoes and gravy, we'd have some of Mother's canned fruit—usually applesauce. Sometimes, for a treat, we had peaches or pears. We also knew we could count on thick slices of Mother's homemade bread.

We didn't have butter, so we smeared our bread with pale yellow oleo.

When kids today complain because they don't have everything they want, they ought to know what life was like when I was a kid. I learned the value of money real quick. I didn't have much, but you don't need much to be happy. You can be happy by doing with what you've got, being safe, getting along with your family, feeling loved. That's being happy.

Yes, life was hard. But my family and me, well, we got by.

Paul McGiness, circa 1938

In a workshop I teach on Life Stories and Legacy Writing, I asked participants to develop a three-generation family map, back to their grandparents' generation, and to list five adjectives or qualities for each of the most important people in their family. At the next session, they were to turn one of those qualities into a story about the family member. Bea Epstein wrote about her father's "naïve innocence" as a result of that exercise. The second part of her story grew out of another exercise. Students were asked to think about the people from whom they learned the most and to write a piece that brought to life a "lesson learned." Of the workshop process, Bea wrote later, "My goal is to develop a series of pieces to give to my children that help recreate the world of my childhood . . . a world that no longer exists. What I have discovered is that the writing itself—the thought, the development, the refinement of the language—is a joyful, creative, and somehow healing experience for me."

—Pat McNees

Fruit Trees Grow in Brooklyn

Bea Epstein

The house I grew up in was the first in a line of small, attached three-family homes. Like any city block, East 94th Street in Brooklyn was all brick, mortar, and concrete. Hidden behind every house was a 30-foot square of potential greenery. Each of these backyard spaces was abandoned—gone to seed or used as storage for the family's discarded junk. In this immigrant, working-class neighborhood, there was precious little time or money to put into a project as frivolous as creating a garden.

Except for my father and his garden.

At the end of each working day, I waited in front of the house, watching for Dad's approaching car. Dad arrived in his painter's cap and overalls, covered with strong-smelling paint, delighted to see me. He unloaded paint cans and cleaned brushes while I chattered on about my day. In the warmer months, we opened the wrought iron garden gate and together checked on Dad's precious trees and bushes. The garden was crowded with large lilac bushes, "snowball trees," a tangle of tea roses, and two large fruit trees—one peach, the other cherry. Those end-of-the-day times were some of the happiest, most precious moments in my father's otherwise unappreciated life.

In the spring, Dad was overjoyed to see his garden flower. He did not seem to notice how few blooms each tree gave forth. He never fertilized or pruned or mulched or did what it actually takes to make a garden grow. Each and every year, no matter the condition of the trees, he imagined a bountiful harvest. Never discouraged, more energized and delighted, he cut a few flowers for me. Then he created a tiny bouquet to take into the kitchen to please his wife.

Busy with the chores of daily life—washing and cleaning, scrubbing and polishing, cooking and baking, Momma had little interest in Dad's offerings, floral or otherwise. His delight and excitement at life's trivia, including his garden, were somehow irritating to her. Her life was consumed with hard work, driven by daily efforts to mold her children and to propel them toward a better future. The joy her husband took in the meager results of the garden he loved seemed somehow misplaced and even foolish to her. His delight seemed only to remind her of how disappointed she was in a life partnership with a naïve, unrealistic husband.

My dad worked his entire life as a house painter. Breathing the paint fumes, climbing the ladders—none of it dampened his playfulness or his delight in the smallest things. He loved pleasing his customers with his handiwork, but most of all, he enjoyed making them laugh. Although Dad's world left little room for enchantment, he consistently found opportunities to interpret life through his unique lens.

There was the time he painted the concrete in our backyard bright green and announced it was "just like having grass." The time he moved the paint cans he used every day as a house painter to one side of the messy garage, set up a lamp and an easy chair someone had abandoned, and declared that the garage was now "the wonderful library he always wanted." All the Sundays Dad drove me to Little Italy to see the beautiful flowers and gardens he loved. There he talked to the Italian immigrants in his Brooklyn version of an Italian accent, tinted with Yiddish—Dad's idea of how to connect with other immigrants.

Dad could take an ordinary situation and spin it into something with a totally different meaning for him. Although part of me was delighted, I understood why Momma found these same qualities maddening. Momma yearned for a more conventional kind of romance. She lost herself in supermarket novels in which the gallant hero charmed his lady-love with his knowledge of her most intimate and secret desires. Momma remained deeply hurt and angry that all Dad's romantic notions had nothing whatsoever to do with who she was or what would truly give her pleasure.

Before she met Dad, Momma had fallen madly in love with a tall, handsome, mysterious man she called "the furrier." Head over heels in love, Momma introduced her young man to Zayde, her father. When Zayde learned that the furrier worked on the Sabbath, he forbade Momma to marry him. Her heart was broken. A few months later, on a sunny day on Brighton Beach, Momma met my curly-headed playful Dad, who was three inches shorter than she. Irving did not work on the Sabbath. Momma married him soon after but never forgave him for not being the furrier.

Late every summer, Dad gathered the tiny harvest yielded by his precious fruit trees—eight or nine insect-free cherries and three or four worm-free peaches. It was then that my parents and I played our parts in the annual family fruit-tree dance.

Dad offers up his harvest to Momma. Will she receive it with good humor and understanding or will she respond with irritation and disappointment? Holding my breath in the final moments of this drama, I see the playfulness in Dad's face. Yet I know that after all the years, he has not really focused on who Momma is, or learned what would

make her happy. I look at Momma's face. I see the pain of disappointment and the yearning for a very different kind of romance.

Bea's parents at a family wedding with Bea, four, and her brother

I wrote this personal history to document my search to identify a book I had read as a child. For more than forty years, I periodically recalled segments of the story. It seemed to hold a strange grip on me, though I had no idea why. Then a series of unlikely coincidences unraveled the mystery behind my attraction to the book and penetrated to the core of who I am, allowing me surprising new insight into my childhood.

—Sandra Diamond Choukroun

The Mysterious Window

Sandra Diamond Choukroun

As a child living in a shady, peaceful Philadelphia neighborhood in 1956, I devotedly borrowed books from the local public library. Reading fiction was my favorite activity. I have no recollection of most of the books I read then, except for one young adult novel that stuck in my mind for decades to come. All I could remember was the main character's older sister traveling to a magical land beyond an isthmus, where people could get "lost," leaving some essential part of themselves behind. The young girl had left a crystal teardrop behind and had not been quite "all there" afterward.

Over the years, I tried on several occasions to find the book again, but without the title or the author's name, it was an impossible quest. Many, many times I conjured the wistful feeling that the book inspired. No matter how I struggled, though, I could never recall more than those few facts. I longed for the magical country, but it was always just beyond the grasp of my conscious mind. I grew up, got married and had two children. They grew up. Years passed between my thoughts of the mysterious book.

Then one day I was in the car en route to an out-of-town bat mitzvah. Ordinarily, I would have been in my own synagogue near home and would not have been listening to a National Public Radio broadcast. As we drove into the parking lot, I heard Harriett Logan of Loganberry Books in Shaker Heights, Ohio, being interviewed. She was explaining that books we read as children often remain in our minds for many years. Only a word or a scenario may be left, much too little to identify the book.

To address the problem, Harriett offers a service called Book Stumper on her bookstore's website (www.logan.com). Members of the public may pay a nominal fee and send her a keyword along with the scenario or information they recall. She then posts the data on the website, where it is viewed by children's librarians from all over the country. Most often, the librarians are able to identify the book, thus offering a special kind of psychic comfort to the searchers.

The next day, I sent my money to Harriett and waited impatiently for the result. A few weeks later, I received a response to my keyword of "isthmus." The book I had spent more than forty years searching for was *The Amazing Vacation* by Dan Wickenden. It was available for sale for eighty dollars. This seemed like a high price, but I decided I couldn't pass it up after such a long wait. I sent a check.

The book arrived a week later. Published in 1956, it had been de-commissioned from a library in Maine and now belonged to me. I was almost wary of reading it after the many years of longing. How would I react? The next weekend, I finally sat down with a cup of tea, opened the shiny cover, and plunged in. Since I am a fast reader, and the book was intended for young people, I finished it in an afternoon.

What a disappointment!

The main character, Joanna, was there, along with her brother Ricky. They were spending a summer vacation at their grandmother's house in the country. The sister I had recalled was actually an older cousin; the crystal teardrop was a turquoise. The story seemed to be a hodgepodge of princesses, porcupines, cowboys, and Indians. Joanna washed dishes and made beds while Ricky rushed around being brave. It was certainly a fable straight from the 1950s. I was shocked that such a book had captured my imagination so powerfully for most of my life. Only one aspect of the story didn't appear hackneyed—the description of the children's access to the magical country. Climbing through a large, stained-glass window, they descended through a mist onto the isthmus where their adventures began.

I put the book away and went back to my adult pursuits. In the back of my mind, though, I reflected not so much on the actual story as on myself. Who had I been in 1956? Why had the story of a window, through which one could lose oneself, been so compelling? Had there been a special window in my history? After a while, the answer came.

I was nine years old when my beloved father became gravely ill. During the six weeks he was hospitalized, my mother managed the family and ran their clinical laboratory business herself. My father was treated at Einstein Medical Center, right across the street from the lab, which we visited often. I was quite familiar with the hospital lawn and the building's many stories and windows. With hopeless resignation, I learned that the hospital had strict rules governing the age of visitors: No children under twelve were admitted. The only option available to my sisters (ages seven and three) and me was to stand outside on the lawn, waving to our father through the window of his room. I don't think he was on a high floor, but to me he looked small and distant. His absence was a profound grief, but only now do I realize its impact. My father returned home pale, too tired for the celebratory chocolate cake we had prepared. Yet he was restored to our family circle and lived to the age of eighty-two.

A year or two after my father's illness, I read Wickenden's book. It left an imprint on my soul, where it remained, lost and sad, until I solved the mystery in my sixth decade. The heart of the mystery had been the window through which a person lost a part of herself, living only partly "there" until the missing jewel was found and returned. In rediscovering and re-reading the book, I finally recognized this traumatic childhood event and experienced a delayed healing that had not been possible before.

Today, *The Amazing Vacation* sits on a special shelf in my bookcase. I am no longer haunted. Although I don't plan to read it often, it's there whenever I feel the need to step through the mist of my own childhood and set foot onto the magical land of my past.

Sandra Choukroun with her parents, long before
"The Mysterious Window"

This is a story about local traditions and the wedding of the parents of Flavia Fernandes, a woman born to a prosperous family of coffee plantation owners in Mangalore, a port city on the west coast of South India. Her mother, Imelda Vaz, and father, Joseph Saldanha, were from a small community of Hindu Brahmin converts to Catholicism, who lived in the area. Their families adopted the Portuguese surnames Vaz and Saldanha upon their conversion to Christianity over three centuries ago. Traditional society prohibited marriage outside the Brahmin Catholic community. Elizabeth Fernandes, Flavia's daughter, commissioned me to write her mother's personal history as a gift on the occasion of her mother's eightieth birthday. This is a selection from Flavia's personal history.

—Ajit Peter Saldanha

A Wedding and an Arrangement

Flavia Fernandes, Narrator

My mother, Imelda Vaz Saldanha, was born on September 18, 1908, near Mangalore, India. She attended local English medium schools wherever her father was posted, until it was deemed proper that she acquire some spit and polish or Anglicized grace and airs. So she and her younger sister, Lila, were sent to the Good Shepherd Convent—a finishing school run by European nuns—in Bellary, India, about two days' journey from Mangalore. Not surprisingly, their companions were European girls and Anglo-Indians. Mum gained an appreciation for western classical music and learned to play the piano, to do needlepoint and embroidery, and about every other skill that would make her a suitable bride for a civil servant. But she was destined to marry the scion of a landowning family.

Mum and Dad first met at a wedding. She was all of twelve years old, petite and radiant with the veneer that finishing school was according her. My father, Joseph Saldanha, was at the more discerning age of nineteen. He must have found her terminally charming, for their meeting inspired innumerable letters, each filled with drawings and jokes. Thoughtful, really, that a nineteen-year-old valued the sensibilities of someone seven years younger. Mum certainly valued the letters, and they stayed with her for a long time. In fact, that is how I became privy to them.

I wasn't the only one privy to those letters. The nuns at Bellary had screened them before passing them on to Mum.

Clearly, they found the letters affectionate and harmless, but they did allow themselves a bit of amusement: "Amy, here's another blue envelope for you."

Almost five years and scores of letters later, Mum and Dad were finally married on May 5, 1925, in Mangalore. It might be unimaginable today, but a twenty-four-year-old marrying a girl of sixteen was commonplace in those days.

Weddings were the biggest of household events at that time, and as my parents were the eldest siblings in their families, no expense was spared. Preparations were made well in advance. Fulltime tailors brought their sewing machines to the house and set up shop to stitch everyone's wedding clothes and Mum's trousseau. Even the goldsmith was brought home to make jewelry.

The grand affair lasted three days.

The first day was the roce [a traditional Hindu ritual, which the community continued to practice after their conversion to Catholicism], which takes place the day before the wedding. The families of the bride and groom hosted separate roce ceremonies in their respective homes, so guests faced difficult choices, as both families were well known in the small community. Mum and Dad wore traditional clothes and were anointed with coconut milk by the elders as the older women sang mournful songs in the Konkani language. These songs, called woyos, lamented the fact that the bride and groom, each lovingly brought up, would soon be leaving their parental homes to start out on their own. Yes, tears were shed all around.

Once the catharsis was over, true to tradition, unrestrained feasting began. Guests who couldn't attend the actual wedding reception for some compelling reason lived it up at the roce. Alcohol flowed like tap water. Cooks were employed for the day to prepare the feast, using in part gifts of fresh produce and live chickens and goats brought the day before by tenants on the family land.

According to tradition, the bride and groom did not see each other after the roce until the wedding two days later. The wedding mass was held on the morning of the third day, followed by a small but extravagant luncheon for close relatives. Evening provided the backdrop for a grand reception. The bridal couple made a magical appearance in a procession led by musicians. An older relative proposed a toast and spoke glowingly about my parents' families. More drinking followed, and dinner was a gourmet's delight. Streams of servers chased each other down rows, between guests seated on the carpeted floor, to ladle out dish after dish of the usual extravaganzas—sorpotel, sannas, sernay sukhey, mutton, pollo, and karam. Guests savored the fare off plantain leaves they had just washed with fresh water.

Dad's sequence of letters had found a befitting finale.

My parents settled down very well into married life. Mum, a delicate and well-groomed person, eased into the unfamiliar landed gentry without discomfort. Ever well dressed, she took great care in choosing the proper saree to wear for social functions. Slim, handsome, and 5 feet 10 inches tall, Dad was equally well dressed. I never saw him wearing anything other than nicely pressed pants and shirts. When on the estate, he wore long stockings and big shoes to guard against leech bites.

Mum's father, Piedade, was very fond of my father. When his daughter Lila was ready for marriage, he sought Dad's assistance. An eligible bachelor called Lawrence

Saldanha, an engineer in the railways, had come to Mangalore from Karachi. His mother's brief was clear: "Find a bride!" The people of Mangalore were agog with the news because Lawrence was a brilliant man with a good job who was deemed to be a gentleman. When the news reached Peidade, he summoned Dad and said, "Joe, I want you to do something for me."

Dad heard him with respectful patience.

"I want you to go and meet this man, Lawrence Saldanha, and try to get him for Lila," Peidade said. Lila was a beautiful girl much sought after by the boys in Mangalore.

When Dad got to Lawrence's house, he saw many cars parked outside and was shocked to find that he was anything but alone in this initiative. He approached the verandah, where several eager ladies were waiting for Lawrence to come out. After greeting the few he knew and nodding courteously to the rest, he walked inside. He scanned various rooms and finally found Lawrence. Surprisingly, the "young man" was actually older than Dad, who was about twenty-six. Lawrence turned out to be thirty-two—twice Lila's age. Unperturbed, Dad introduced himself and asked, "Lawrence, do you know there are many people waiting for you outside?"

"Yes, I know. That's why I haven't been outside."

"You come with me in my car," Dad said. "I will take you to meet someone really beautiful!"

Utterly taken with Dad's boldness, Lawrence followed him to the car, walking past all the waiting ladies and into a delightfully unexpected future.

Lila and Lawrence met on April 3rd, became engaged the next day, and married on April 28th. They had seven children, each born in what later became Pakistan. The family eventually immigrated *en masse* to Canada.

Today, arranged marriages appear to have fallen out of favor. Young men and women like to manage their own affairs. Commendable, no doubt, but this approach has its disadvantages: The field of search is narrow, much is left to chance meetings, and it's up to the couple to make it work without much social help. Arranged marriages emerged from a sense of social obligation. Many people who understood the prospective families came to be involved in the arrangement and felt responsible for it after the marriage took place. Because of this networking, the field of search was vast, and it was possible for a girl from Mangalore to marry a man from Karachi. Although I understand that far more unlikely marriages now emerge as a result of the Internet, I wonder if they come with any form of social protection.

Flavia Saldanha Fernandes (far left), age five, in 1931, celebrating her First Holy Communion in Mangalore, India, with her father, mother, and two sisters

George McCoy was eighty-three when he told me his story. I first met him at a family gathering, and I noticed that he kept nodding off while the family chatted about their activities and events. Periodically, he would open his eyes and exclaim, "That reminds me of the time when…" Off he would go, coming to life as he recounted (I'm sure for the umpteenth time) one of his war stories. George was eighteen years old when he enlisted with the Royal Hamilton Light Infantry (RHLI) and soon found himself in a trench in France. He is a wonderful storyteller, and it was a privilege and a pleasure to capture his stories and preserve them in a book. George currently lives in a nursing home in Dundas, Ontario, Canada.

—Gillian Hewitt

Fear, Fatigue, and Misery

George McCoy, Narrator

We were supposed to go to France on D-Day plus six [June 12, 1944], but there was a storm in the channel, so we left from Newhaven on July 4, almost a month later than planned.

We were transported over by an American ship. The Americans didn't like us much because it was the Fourth of July, and they had planned a nice night in the pub. When word came in that they had to take the RHLI into France, they were very unhappy. They got us to France nicely, though. We walked ashore and never even got our feet wet.

After landing, we marched about five miles inland and spent the night in a farmer's field. We were told never to go into any buildings because they could be booby-trapped; another reason was that we could get lice. It rained that first night, and most of the guys from this one company moved into the barn to get out of the rain. By morning, they were scratching themselves to death. The medical officer lined them up, stripped from the waist down. He had a big paintbrush and a bucket of potassium permanganate, and he would lather them front and back as each guy went by. It was the funniest thing I ever saw.

Before we saw real battle, we did a lot of singing. We marched in the daytime and got to our position about dusk. Everybody was happy and singing, but after we started getting casualties, we never sang again.

The first position we took in France was in an orchard. It was what we called a holding position—not attacking anybody, just sitting there being mortared to death. We moved in at night, and that was our baptism by fire, where we had our first casualties. I can still hear the scream for "Stretcher bearers!" It made me realize this was it; this was the real McCoy. *We're not shooting blanks anymore.*

The slit trench became our home in France. We each had a blanket; if it got wet, it got wet. We put branches and sod over our trench to make a roof, leaving only a small spot for entry and exit. We got mortared heavily. Sometimes, if we came under fire very suddenly, we would do a shell scrape—a trench only 12 inches deep. It at least gave us some protection from enemy fire.

Living in a slit trench was tricky. I found that out the first time I had to go to the john. I got out and went by a hedgerow. The Germans began lacing the area with mortar fire from about 700 to 800 yards away. When the mortar fire started, I realized I couldn't run very fast with my pants down. Those times when it wasn't safe to go out, you had to use one end of your slit trench for a toilet. Not very pleasant, but better than getting killed.

A few times, I was able to spare enough of my water to shave. Filling a mess tin with a pint of water, I would have a wash and a shave, then wash my feet. The water was almost like mud by the time I finished, but I felt better. That was how the infantry lived on the front line.

Our rations were set up in boxes with different canned food, including steak and kidney pies, bacon, hard tack biscuits, and so on. I loved steak and kidney pie. Luckily for me, none of the other guys in my section did, so I had all I wanted. I heated them up in my mess tin at one end of my slit trench. We used Tommy cookers—little tablets of a compound that would burn—to heat a mess tin full of stew in very short order. I was hungry as hell one day and had just heated up a can of steak and kidney pie when a mortar hit the roof of my slit trench. About ten pounds of earth came at me. I just scraped the earth off and ate like the devil. It was a little gritty, but it was good.

A few days later, our colonel [the late Brigadier-General Denis Whitaker] was hit. He was evacuated right away, and they had to bring in another colonel. I saw a jeep coming down the dirt road, and the Germans started to mortar the area. The mortars were getting pretty close to the jeep, so I jumped in my hole. The next thing I know, a pair of boots came in on top of me. Inside those boots was my brother! He was a captain in the brigade, and he and the brigadier were bringing Lieutenant-Colonel Rockingham into the front lines to replace Denis Whitaker.

"If you think I'm going to stand up and salute you, you're crazy," I said.

My brother knew I was somewhere out there, but didn't know exactly where. He just jumped into a hole, and it happened to be mine. That was a nice little meeting we had. Later, Tim and I were wounded at the Seine River, one mile and one day apart. We were evacuated to the same hospital in England.

I was only at the front for two months. A lot of people talk about the front. Maybe they are five miles from it, where the stores areas are, but right at the actual front—

that was where the colonel and everybody lived. As Denis Whitaker wrote in his book, *Victory at Falaise*, battle fatigue was caused by fear, fatigue, and misery over a period of time.

Fear? Everybody was afraid. If they said they weren't, they were lying.

Fatigue? We would go days without a night's sleep. Instead, we would catnap or take turns napping if there were two in a trench.

Misery? We lived in misery. We were constantly thinking a mortar would come into the trench and wipe us out. If one came into your trench, you wouldn't know about it. All they did was shovel the dirt in, and that was your grave because there wouldn't be enough left of you.

Pvt. George McCoy,
Royal Hamilton Light Infantry

After my mother, Mary Spencer Kimball McLean, fell off her horse Sandy in September 1999 at the age of seventy-eight, she was miserable. To divert her from the pain and outrage of broken bones, and to keep her quiet, I began interviewing Mother about her life and then transcribing her stories. She died in 2005. I published her personal history, A Life on Horseback, *in 2006.*

—Cynthia K. McLean

George S. Patton, A Gentleman General

Mary Spencer Kimball McLean, Narrator

In Paris, to repair my reputation as a good worker, I immediately signed up with a local American Red Cross (ARC) canteen, while most of the girls toured the sights and partied. Within two weeks, I was recalled to join the Group L Clubmobile stationed with General George Patton's Third Army in Germany. [Clubmobiles were Red Cross service clubs on wheels that provided free doughnuts and coffee to servicemen at American bases or camps.] I arrived in early December 1944 and was assigned to the Sioux Falls Clubmobile, which was captained by Jean Gordon, General Patton's niece.

Not long after I arrived, I was invited to accompany Jean to dinner at Patton's headquarters. The general was a true gentleman! He never used cuss words in front of women and always stood up when a lady entered the room. Not all generals, however, were as disciplined as Patton. I will always remember a party he hosted for General Eisenhower. Ike got drunk, as did another Red Cross girl. I can see her now, sitting on Ike's lap, cooing to him and patting his bald head. I was so disgusted that I refused to vote for Eisenhower when he later ran for president. I still thought men my father's age should be gentlemen.

The press attacked Patton's reputation every chance it got. He refused to let reporters on the front lines because he distrusted their discretion and worried that they would write reports giving the Germans clues to our troop movements. The press crucified him when he slapped a shell-shocked soldier in Sicily. The general had been awarding Purple Heart medals to wounded soldiers in the hospital wards and was badly shaken by what he had seen. Patton lost it when he asked a weeping boy what his problem was and the young soldier answered, "Scared!"

With his pearl-handled pistols and spit-and-polish riding boots, General Patton could be quite intimidating. Underneath the gruffness, however, I found a kind and caring person. He knew how to lead troops and talked to them in their own (sometimes crude) language. Yes, he was strict, but I admired this as much as I admired my mother's strictness. His men knew he would never ask them to take risks that he was unwilling to take. If a death occurred in one of his soldiers' families, he was the first to know about it and, even when under fire, would try to tell the soldier himself.

The general seemed to like me, and I loved his cavalry

stories about riding with General John J. Pershing on the 1916 Punitive Expedition against Pancho Villa in Mexico. I did, however, get in trouble with Patton once when a GI in Luxembourg traded me a small German motorcycle for a few packs of cigarettes. I brought my new toy back in our Clubmobile and decided to ride it from our living quarters to the ARC garage, to show off to my friends. I had hardly gunned the motor when Patton came stomping over. *Didn't I know that gas was rationed?* he scolded. Then he said that he too had been given a motorcycle, and he challenged me to a race, after which both cycles would become the property of the U.S. Army. Needless to say, he won.

Mother closely followed my adventures during the war. She had been offered the job of U.S. liaison with the ARC in England, but there was no way she could leave Daddy. She remained in Watertown, New York, as chairman of the Jefferson County chapter of the Red Cross. She wrote Patton about me, and he wrote her back. I found his letter with all my war correspondence when I came home in 1945. Unfortunately, most of my war letters aren't worth rereading. Patton warned us repeatedly against leaking information to the enemy, so I never mentioned precisely where I was or with which army unit. I also have no photographs of myself with the general. He refused to pose with any woman, for fear the press would sensationalize the relationship back home.

Not long before the Germans surrendered in May 1945, Patton was sent to liberate Buchenwald, one of the Nazis' biggest concentration camps. It essentially was a photo-op to publicize Nazi atrocities; reporters and photographers from around the world were there. Fearful that the enlisted men might start killing off SS guards after witnessing the horrors, Patton decided to take the Red Cross in with him to "normalize" the situation. Jean Gordon, Betty South, and I spent several hours outside the gates handing out coffee and doughnuts.

You could smell that damned concentration camp from miles away. Germans lined the roads, wailing that they had not known what was going on at the camp. I was so angered by their dishonest blindness that if I'd had a gun, I might have used it. We saw piles of dead bodies, covered in lime, in open ditches. We saw the ovens where the Nazis had incinerated thousands of prisoners. We watched the barely alive crawl out of filthy sheds, only to die at our feet. It was sickening. Afterwards, General Patton gave each of us four battle stars to wear. He felt we deserved them for all we had seen and done.

During the summer of 1945, my Red Cross unit remained busy feeding and entertaining troops slowly being sent home. I also had time for sightseeing in the rolling German countryside, including a visit to Adolf Hitler's Crow's Nest in the southern Alps, where some GIs and I "liberated" a couple of bottles of port from Hitler's private stock. The boys took me white-water rafting, and I rode with "Hap" Gay on lovely horses given to Patton by the Russians, who had stolen them from the Germans. I only wish I could have ridden one of the Lippizan horses General Patton saved from destruction.

Despite what the newspapers reported about him, I didn't experience Patton as an arrogant egomaniac. During

the summer of 1945, I accompanied him and a group of officers on a boat trip around one of the mountain lakes. The
officers were fawning over him, which he indeed loved.
When he pulled out his revolver and took out a duck with
one shot, they all cheered, congratulating him on his
marksmanship. Unfortunately, it was a diving duck. Sitting
in the back of the boat, I saw it pop up after we had cruised
by, so I tapped Patton on the sleeve and whispered what I
had seen. He whispered back that I had seen *"no such thing."*
I saw his mouth twitch with a smile as he turned to rejoin
the officers' conversation.

Patton publicly declared that after mopping up Europe,
he wanted to go to China and finish off the "Japs." We all
wanted to go with him! This, of course, came to nothing
when the Americans dropped bombs on Hiroshima and
Nagasaki in August. At that point, I told Don that I would
marry him in Europe. ARC headquarters gave me permission to marry and to be attached to Don's Army outfit until
he could be sent home in 1946, and General Patton agreed
to take me down the aisle in Daddy's absence.

When my Clubmobile came home one evening in early
September after a week in the mountains with an ack-ack
(anti-aircraft artillery) unit, General Patton and his aide,
Major Pat Merle-Smith, were waiting for me. Patton beck-
oned me into the library, where he informed me as best he
could that my mother had been killed in a car accident in
Watertown.

Driving a Red Cross station wagon, Mother had been
headed to a child-care center she had set up with federal
funds to allow women to work during the war. On the way,

she had stopped off to tell her former housekeeper, Florence, that arrangements had been made for the body of Florence's only son to be brought home for burial. This was a boy Mother had encouraged to graduate from high school and to join the U.S. Coast Guard; he became one of their youngest captains ever. The young man had been killed overseas when a drunken sailor shot him during a brawl. After a short visit with Florence, Mother drove across town. She pulled out to cross Bellew Avenue, but misjudged the speed of a tractor-trailer full of oil, which slammed into her right front fender. The station wagon spun around, and she was thrown 29 feet onto the pavement. She died instantly.

General Patton told me that I must go home to be with my father. I said, "No, sir, I want to stay with my friends."

He said, "That's fine, but I'll have a plane take you to Paris tomorrow at 6:00 a.m."

I protested but was on that plane the following morning and returned to Watertown two days later.

Quentin Brown and fellow crewmember Bob Giles became World War II POWs after their B-17 was shot down over Berlin on April 18, 1944. They remained in captivity until the war ended thirteen months later. In 2001, Mr. Brown asked me to help him publish his war stories. The following excerpt from his resulting book, There I Was at 30,000 Feet, *describes two people he met in Berlin who helped him survive the ordeals of captivity. His close friendship with them and with Bob Giles continued after the war.*

—Marion Johnson

Beacons of Light in a Dark Time

Quentin Brown, Narrator

April 19, 1944

I don't remember the ride across Berlin to our destination—the Hermann Göring Luftwaffen Lazarett Nummer Acht, where Bob Giles, two badly wounded Allied airmen, and I were transported to a second-floor room in the 500-year-old military complex. Six thousand miles from home and badly injured, I was worried about my aging parents and really missed my wife. A bleak and indefinite future lay ahead of me. Except for Bob, I had no one to turn to for reassurance and support.

Then I met Maria Lorenzen and Guy Rogers.

Maria Lorenzen, circa 1944

Schwester[1] Maria needs a Hemingway to do her justice. She was, I believe, one of the great characters of the times. I first learned her name in that second-floor room as I watched her talk quietly and soothingly to Guy Rogers, another wounded flyer, while she peeled and cut apples into eighths for him. This made me think even less of Guy, of course. Why should he get all that special treatment? It was my third day in Germany, and no one had given me an apple!

Some days later, I learned that Guy had the greatest cause for complaint of anyone in the room. Shot down on March 6, 1944, during the first daylight raid on Berlin, Guy had to have one of his legs amputated. His face was so severely burned that his mouth could only form a small round opening about the size of a fountain pen. Schwester Maria had to find food for him that could be administered in very small slices.

Guy and I lay head-to-toe in our respective hospital beds for days. Flat on our backs with nothing to read and nothing to do, we talked and learned a lot about each other. In spite of his condition, he never stopped saying, "What a

---

[1]A German Wehrmacht Army term for head nurse.

great life. How lucky we are!"
Guy always managed to get me
thinking about the positive,
about the lives we both would
have when the war was over.

Schwester Maria also lifted my spirits. Every morning
just after seven, she blew into
our room and greeted us with a
cheery, "Gut morgen! Raus,
raus!"(Good morning! Rise
and shine!) To let in some
fresh air, she threw open the
windows overlooking a grassy
park-like area. Blowing a half-
inch strand of yellow hair out
of her eye, she would cheerily

*Guy Rogers, 1944, before he was
shot down during the first
daylight raid on Berlin*

take everyone's temperature, check our bandages, and fluff
our pillows. But she refused to hear any complaints of sickness or pain. "Ach! You not sick, you fine! You be good,"
she would state derisively. Maria never allowed us to feel
sorry for ourselves. She had a nickname for each of us... I
was "My Brownie," Guy Rogers was "My Row-gerrh," and
an English boy named Ken Davis, who really liked cheese,
was "Cheese Davis."

Maria's straw-colored hair was tied back in a tight bun,
and her face was ruddy. At the time, I thought she was fifty
or sixty years old and likened her to my mother. And, oh,
how I needed a mother! True, I had a wonderful wife whom
I loved dearly and missed so much, but Ruth had loved and

cared for me only one year. I needed a mother. Maria, I believe, became that symbol for me.

Even on her busiest mornings, Maria always stopped next to my bed and looked up at the two framed, black and white pictures that hung on the wall behind me. The photo on the left was that of Adolph Hitler, the one on the right, Hermann Göring. The Allied world had seen that picture of Göring many times. Smiling and jovial in his fully adorned Reichmarshal's tunic, Göring had a confident glint in his eye that supposedly captivated the ladies. Hitler, on the other hand, looked down with a dictatorial scowl. Looking up at the Reichmarshal, Maria would say, "Allo, my Hermann!" Then turning her face to the left, "Ach, Ich vergessen! Allo, Herr Hitler." She was obviously much fonder of "her Hermann."

Maria never mentioned politics or the war. Maybe that was because she had been to the United States. Like so many Germans after World War I, Maria's poverty-stricken parents sent her to America so they would have one less mouth to feed. "Papa say two girls on a farm too many," she told me. She came to Chicago in 1933 and lived there for a short time with her brother. From 1933 until 1936, she worked as an au pair. She had to leave that job when she received word that her father was very sick.

Back at home on her family's beloved farm at Langeness, one of the Friesian Islands in the North Sea, Maria lost any thoughts of a return to Chicago and the land of opportunity. Her father died soon after her return, and she had to take over the small farm. Eventually, she was called away from the farm by the Nazi government. She completed nurse's training (practically nonexistent before Hitler's regime) and was immediately assigned to Flensburg on the Baltic coast of Schleswig-Holstein, where Hitler was secretly producing world-class submarines three years before the war.

When asked about Germany, Maria told her patients she was very proud of her homeland. Yet with all of her admiration for "Herr Hitler" and "My Hermann," she did her best to make us so-called "Luftgangsters in Hermann's Place" as comfortable and happy as possible. She often brought us leftover food from her "too sick" Luftwaffen pilots. If other wounded Germans didn't eat their allotted rations, Maria would sneak the remainder to us as well. When our room was overfilled with newly wounded American flyers, those who could walk were allowed to visit other rooms on the floor.

Maria saved Guy Rogers' life. After he was shot down, Guy lay in the hospital for many days with his left leg broken in two places, six inches below his hip. It was a compound fracture. With nothing but paper bandages, very little sulfa, and no penicillin, infection set in. The German doctors wanted to amputate at once, but Maria pledged that she would nurse him. Her superiors said she hadn't the time… There were too many wounded Germans and Allies. When Maria pleaded that she would use her own time, they tried to save Guy's leg by giving him blood transfusions from other wounded POWs. But they eventually ran out of his blood type, and the infection grew worse. On one of Maria's late-night rounds, she found Guy looking gaunt, with sunken cheeks. "Very gray," she later said. She roused the

Stopsartz (head doctor), who removed the leg around 4:00 a.m. Guy was out of danger by the time Bob and I arrived.

Maria also pleaded for my arm. The head of the German hospital, Dr. Frahnk, told me that a major nerve had been severed. Compassionate in tone, he was also businesslike and to the point. The arm, he said, could atrophy and at best be a cold, useless appendage. The Germans had many civilian and military wounded; doctors, medication, and bandages were at a premium. With a quick "cleaver" job, a prisoner could be moved to a convalescent area. When Dr. Frahnk recommended amputation, Maria pledged to nurse me on her own time if necessary. He agreed to wait a few days. Thanks to Maria and no infection, I have a near perfect arm today.

Maria never expressed any hatred toward the Allies for attacking her country. A few days after I arrived at Hermann Göring's place, she mentioned without wrath, "We have some sher schlect (seriously wounded) Hitlerjugend[2] upstairs. Their country military school was hit with bombs." Suddenly, I remembered seeing a bombed-out building with a red tile roof just before I landed in the hayfield. My stomach turned over as she spoke, and I wondered, *Were those my bombs?*

---

[2] One of a series of youth organizations designed to mobilize, politically indoctrinate, and provide pre-military training to young men ages 14 to 18 in the German Third Reich.

Though Schwester Maria Lorenzen loved her Germany, she was a nurse first. After that, she was a German and a loyal soldier. Maria loved her sick German boys, but she also loved her "Tommies." She and Guy Rogers were my beacons of light during a very dark time.

Reunited in Germany in 1972, Quentin Brown and Maria Lorenzen (pictured above at Maria's home in 1987) met five times on Maria's island, Langeness, before she died in 2000

My father has long regaled our family with harrowing tales of his service as a submarine officer in the Pacific during World War II. Like many others, I listened intently to those stories and thought, "Some day, we should record them." I realized they were something special when I decided to give a speech about my dad's submarine adventures to a local Toastmasters group. As I practiced the speech on my then-teenaged daughter, her mouth dropped open and her eyes widened. I figured if a story could mesmerize a jaded teenager, it was a pretty good one. Fortunately, I was able to preserve many of my dad's World War II stories and photographs in a book we all treasure.

—Jeanne S. Archer

Through a Periscope

Jack Smalling, Narrator

Just eleven days before our submarine, *The Spearfish*, left Saipan during World War II, our U.S. task forces had begun attacking Luzon, making us keenly aware that Japanese reinforcements on their way to the Philippines were likely to be traveling in the same waters.

Our assignment was photographic reconnaissance of the beaches of Iwo Jima, in preparation for a landing by our Marine invasion force scheduled for February 1945. Taking Iwo Jima was critical because of its proximity to mainland Japan. The island would provide a safe landing field for any damaged U.S. bombers and a base of support for our bombers flying back and forth to Japan. Though American aircraft would also conduct photoreconnaissance, our submarine's cameramen would be able to provide critical close-up views of the beaches before our forces went ashore.

As we cruised the eight hundred miles or so from Saipan to Iwo Jima, we felt some comfort in the fact that our submarine sailed inside a "security box." That meant we were within a "no attack" zone of fifty miles ahead, one hundred miles behind, and fifty miles on each side of our track. In addition, an order had been issued not to attack any lone ship or submarines near Iwo Jima. The orders seemed pretty clear. With so many "do not attack" orders, meant to protect people like us, we should have been safe. But we weren't.

Early in the morning of November 29, 1944, we approached Iwo Jima. To conserve our batteries, we had intended to travel on the surface to within a few miles of the southeast beach before submerging. There was a full moon and a calm sea with phosphorescent water that left a trail in our wake—not ideal for stealth. Our ship was an easy target for bombers; all they had to do was follow our glistening trail. We were alert and didn't trust anyone. Submarines treat all aircraft as a potential enemy. But we didn't expect what came next.

U.S. Navy officer Jack Smalling

During our approach, we monitored many frequencies of radio traffic, including those of the American forces. We were shocked to intercept a transmission about our own bombers sighting a ship—*us!* They had been briefed that we would be there, and it had not been difficult for them to spot our neon wake. One of the pilots radioed the others, "It's not a ship; it's a submarine."

The next thing we heard was, "Let's bomb the bastard anyway."

Not a nice thing to call us! We immediately took evasive action and made an emergency dive. The bombs from those U.S. aircraft passed just over our sub, narrowly missing us. Some said the bombs passed within 75 feet. Too close! We were shaken but not damaged, just a bit angry. We didn't really think we were "bastards."

After that excitement, we proceeded toward Iwo Jima to take photographs along the southern shore of the island from east to west and around the western tip. We were warned to look out for mines. How can you do that? Fortunately, we didn't find any. We spent the day taking pictures with two cameras, alternating our two periscopes so that we could get a panoramic view of the entire coastline for the landing craft.

Lining the beaches were numerous caves where Japanese soldiers could hide their artillery from enemy aircraft. Through our periscopes, we could clearly see the soldiers at the entrance to the caves near Mt. Surbachi—an extinct volcano on the southwest tip of Iwo Jima.

That night after completing the first round of photographs, we moved away from the island to surface and recharge our batteries. We heard over the radio that the bombers had reported hitting and sinking a submarine. The Pacific Command, knowing where we were supposed to be, figured that our submarine had been the target. We couldn't immediately correct that error since our assignment included maintaining radio silence while near Iwo Jima. We were not to transmit until we had finished our mission. When he heard news of our reported demise, the

Commander of Submarines in the Pacific radioed our ship, ordering us to report the results from the attack just as soon as we cleared the island. His request went unanswered.

While developing the pictures taken that day, we discovered that one of our cameras had malfunctioned. Once again, we would have to approach the coast and take more pictures in order to complete our mission. So the Commander of the Pacific Fleet spent two more days biting his fingernails.

As we approached Iwo Jima on December 1 to retake the photos along the southern coast, we again were attacked by American bombers. Again, they missed us by about 75 feet. It was getting to be a bad habit.

The second series of photographs was excellent, but we had another series to take along the western coast. Luckily, we were not attacked on the third run, and we were able to safely surface in darkness and develop the pictures. They were acceptable. On the morning of December 3rd, we headed away from Iwo Jima and back to Saipan to deliver the photographs and finally report to our commander about the success of our mission and the unsuccessful attacks of the bombers on our submarine.

"There was no damage except to pride," we reported.

Later, we heard that the bomber pilots had been court-martialed for their attacks on our submarine. This may seem a bit harsh, but they had disobeyed their orders not to attack any single ship or submarine near the island. They should have been thankful that they didn't sink us. **We** sure were.

Jack Smalling (1990) on a submarine like the one he
served on in the Pacific during World War II

In 2002, I researched and wrote In Good Conscience, *a book about people who helped Japanese-Americans affected by the internment during World War II. The personal histories of these ordinary heroes shed light on what inspires some to take action, when so many others turn their backs. The Hannan family's story evolved from interviews, excerpts from Helen Hannan's memoirs, letters and journals written by Nell and Mari Hannan, and Mari's photo album.*

—Shizue Siegel

"The Hannan Family" is reprinted from In Good Conscience: Supporting Japanese Americans During the Internment *by Shizue Siegel, published in 2006 by the Asian American Curriculum Project (AACP, Inc.), with support from the California Civil Liberties Public Education Program and The Military Intelligence Service Association of Northern California.*

The Hannan Family:
A Living Civics Lesson

Shizue Siegel

After the war in Europe ended, in 1945, Maj. Lawrence J. Hannan was released from active duty. He could easily have reclaimed the job that had been held open for him at a Chicago law firm and returned with his family to their comfortable, suburban bungalow. Instead, he took his wife, Nell, and their three children to the wilds of Colorado and went to work as a project lawyer at a Japanese-American internment camp.

His daughter Helen, twelve at the time and now seventy, explained, "Nearly 120,000 Japanese Americans had been herded into internment camps due to wild hysteria and racial prejudice at the start of the war. Papa thought this was a disgraceful act and most shameful. Not one of these people was ever known to act in any way disloyally.

"As far as I know, he didn't know any Japanese-Americans before he went to the internment camp. But as a lawyer, he recognized that a great crime had been done by the government against its own citizens, in violation of the 'due process of law' guaranteed by the Constitution. They had been imprisoned without being accused of a crime, simply because they looked like the enemy."

Lawrence Hannan held very strong moral convictions and acted upon them. His military career had stalled after he defended a young Jewish soldier whom he believed to be the victim of anti-Semitism. "My father got him declared innocent in the court martial," declared Helen, "but at the cost of all hope of his own advancement in the Army. The general made his life miserable and was determined to be rid of him."

Nell Hannan shared her husband's sense of social justice. A devout Catholic, she felt fortunate compared with her own mother, who had been sent to work at a rope factory in England at the age of four while caring for her invalid mother. The tales of her mother's Dickensian sufferings instilled a deep sense of compassion in Nell. At the height of the Depression, when her husband's law office cut his hours and salary in half, she was grateful that he had a job at all. She kept a bottomless pot of soup on the stove to feed hungry strangers who knocked on the back door. They were not "bums," she explained to her children, but hardworking men who had lost their jobs.

Nell's heritage included courage as well as compassion. Her maternal great-great-grandfather, Thomas Duffy, and his brother had been schoolteachers in Ireland in the 1830s. When the British made it a capital crime to teach Irish children to read and write, the Duffy brothers became hedge masters—teachers who hid in hedgerows and ditches while teaching on the sly. With the British hot on their trail, the Duffys changed their name and went underground in England. It would be three generations before the family felt safe enough to reclaim the Duffy name.

Full of high ideals and lively curiosity, the Hannans arrived at the internment camp at Amache, Colorado, in July 1945. "It was desolate and barren," Helen recalled. "Dust and sand blew constantly, and you could look for miles in all directions and see nothing."

While the internees were squeezed, up to seven to a room, in tarpaper barracks without bathrooms, kitchens, or running water, the five Hannans were assigned the relative luxury of a three-bedroom apartment. "The staff had their own little world," explained Helen, "literally with a white picket fence around it. They had little white cottages with green grass around a sort of little village square, plunked down in the midst of this desolation. And they kept themselves that way, by and large." Most of the staff were, in Helen's words, "of the bureaucratic mindset; they were there to do a job and get paid to do it. They did not mingle with the people from the 'colony.' Some of the staff had almost what would amount to a bad attitude."

"The neighboring town of Granada," she continued, "was very hostile to anyone from the camp. The people there went out of their way to be unaccommodating." The bank refused to open an account for Lawrence Hannan because he worked at Amache. The drugstore hid magazines under the counter and sold them only to the locals.

In contrast, the Hannans and the internees quickly befriended each other. "We just sort of took to each other," Helen recalled. "The day we got to Amache was Mari's birthday. The servers in the mess hall were girls from the colony, and somehow they got wind of it. They came over to wish her a happy birthday. She began talking to them, and they became lifelong friends."

The family joined the internees for mass at the camp's Catholic church. Soon Mari was assisting Father Swift, a Maryknoll missionary who had served in Korea before the war.

The entire family tried to learn Japanese, Nell reported. "At home, we have a big blackboard on one side of our kitchen, and it's covered with Japanese. The rest of us try. We can't seem to keep up with Mari."

"Mari was a sixteen-year-old girl," said Helen, "who should have been thinking about boys and makeup and

Mari Hannan, sixteen, when she and her family went to live at a Japanese-American internment camp

clothes, but she was totally engrossed in the lives of the internees and what she could do for them. She practically had a daycare center in our house. All these little ones would be down in our quarters all day, playing board games and card games like 'Fish' and making French-fried potatoes. I don't think we endeared ourselves to the staff for associating with the internees; they kept their distance. But Mari was a real mother hen to the Japanese children.

"Mari used to gather up as many children as she could stuff into our father's convertible and take them into Granada for ice cream cones and a trip to the town wading pool. It had never entered the head of anybody on the staff that they might take some of these little kids into town for a little frolic, until Mari came along. Everybody was dumbfounded. The other mothers did not want their children in the wading pool with the Japanese children, as if something was going to rub off. They would glare and make remarks about people who didn't belong there, and who ought to go back where they came from. But Mari didn't care. I sort of felt like Joan of Arc's little sister. She forged on into battle, and I'd be standing there in amazement."

In December 1944, the U.S. Supreme Court decided that the government could not hold "concededly loyal" persons against their will, and the West Coast was reopened to Japanese–Americans in January 1945. The internees were free to leave the camps, but many of them hesitated. They had been forcibly evicted from their homes and lost most of their possessions. After three years of incarceration, many were afraid to venture from the camps into an uncertain future.

Only two weeks after the Hannans arrived at Amache, Nell wrote, "It has been decided by the powers that be that Amache is to be the first camp to close. Larry might not have taken the job had he known, but we wouldn't have missed it for the world." Offered his pick of assignments, Hannan asked to be transferred to another internment camp.

During the next three months, Nell Hannan wrote, "We stand by and watch the camp fold up around us. The internees are free to go, and the sooner the better the organization will like it. Most of them are very nice people, and they are only staying because they can't get possession of their property or a place to live."

In August, news came that the Pacific war was over. Helen recalled, "While there had been wild rejoicing on VE Day, we didn't celebrate VJ Day in camp. We knew many people who had lost family members in the atomic bombings, and it seemed indecent to rejoice under the circumstances. We were all just quietly grateful that it was over."

Amache closed on October 15, 1945. Two weeks later, the Hannans arrived at the Tule Lake Segregation Center in California. Lawrence Hannan again was to serve as a project attorney; however, the Hannans soon found that Tule Lake was very different. Over the next six months, they would see thousands of "disloyal" internees forcibly deported to Japan, including almost three thousand U.S. citizens, two-thirds of them children. Lawrence and Nell worked tirelessly to help the internees avoid deportation, but there was little they could do.

Of those difficult days, Helen Hannan said, "The internment was so wrong. The little bit that you could do felt like you were putting your thumb in the dike, but our family believed that you had to do what you could. And the people were so appreciative. They could tell that Papa really cared about them. For years afterwards, they would visit him and bring fruit, veggies, flowers, even live chickens!"

After the Tule Lake Segregation Center closed, the Hannans moved to Sacramento, California, where Lawrence Hannan went to work for the U.S. Bureau of Reclamations. Helen reported that until his death in 1964, "He was still going around with his antennae up for any injustices."

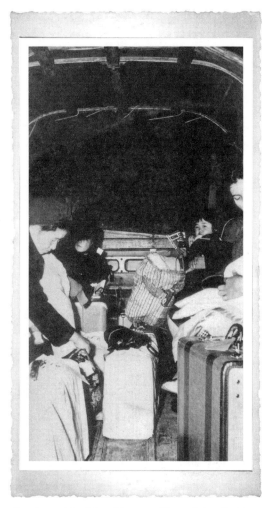

*Barely visible, Mari Hannan (far right) riding in a
truck with Japanese-American friends threatened
with deportation in the waning days of the
Tule Lake Segregation Center*

Stories about people make an institution's history come to life and help dramatize what makes the place tick. On Monday mornings, vans carry patients from three airports to the campus of the National Institutes of Health (NIH) in Bethesda, Maryland. At the heart of that campus sits Building 10, the NIH Clinical Center—a research hospital and clinic where patients from all over the nation, and in some cases the world, receive cutting-edge medical care. Other hospitals do research, but one-half the research beds in the United States are in Building 10. Patients do not pay for medical treatment at NIH because they are there as "patient volunteers." The following selection is from Building Ten at Fifty, which brings the center's history to life through stories about patients, physician-scientists, and nurses, based on 105 interviews. All of the men in this story except Charles Meredith were doctors doing research for the National Cancer Institute, one of many institutes that would conduct clinical research (research involving human patients) in the Clinical Center. Major break-throughs in cancer research came fairly early in Building 10, but the protocols that brought them were not whole-heartedly welcomed at the time.

—Pat McNees

"Pioneering in Chemotherapy" is reprinted from Building Ten at Fifty: 50 Years of Clinical Research at the NIH Clinical Center, copyright © 2003 by Pat McNees.

Pioneering in Chemotherapy

Pat McNees

R oy Hertz admitted the NIH Clinical Center's first patient—Charles Meredith, a Maryland farmer with prostate cancer—on July 6, 1953. Since then, NIH investigators have seen more than a quarter million patients. As protocols changed so did the diseases the nurses would see on the wards. In 1953, polio patients in respirators got special care from nurses on the eleventh floor. When an effective vaccine came along, polio was no longer an active protocol. But cancer was always there.

These were the early days of single-agent chemotherapy, and the side effects of drugs were "pretty rough," says Leonard Fenninger, an early researcher there. The NIH had a special arrangement with the United Mine Workers (before they built their own hospitals), through which the union would refer children with untreated leukemia to the Clinical Center. "We had a number of children who came out of the hollows of West Virginia, who had never been away from home, whose mothers came with them, and *they* had never been away from home." The mothers were used to death in the mines, but they were also used to tremendous community support. In Bethesda, they were completely removed from that, except for the doctors, nurses, and social workers at the Clinical Center. By the end of that first year, all but one of the thirty-two patients Fenninger saw were dead. He decided he couldn't divorce himself from the people he was caring for, whom he felt were doomed to die. In 1954, he left the NIH.

There was tremendous opposition to the Clinical Center's experiments in chemotherapy, especially with a population of beautiful young children. The children's deaths produced major emotional stress, not only for the parents but for everybody around them. "And there had always been a feeling that you really shouldn't interfere with God's will," says Fenninger. Meanwhile, Jim Holland, Fenninger, and others got the National Cancer Institute (NCI) labs up and running so that everything was in place when a more successful intervention came along.

A young Chinese postdoctoral medical fellow, Min Chiu Li, brought from the Sloan-Kettering some women with gestational choriocarcinoma—a rapidly fatal and rare cancer of fetal tissue of the placenta. Ann Plunkett, one of the first nurses on the cancer service, recalls, "They would come in, these young women, and die within a matter of weeks to months." Li proposed administering large doses of a new folic acid antagonist, known now as methotrexate, and Roy Hertz allowed Li to decide for himself whether to proceed. At first, the drug made the patients ill. Then one patient responded, and a second, and a third. "It made you a real believer in medical research, to see these young women begin to live," says Plunkett. In 1957, through the use of single-agent chemotherapy, the medical team had achieved not just remission, but a cure—the first successful chemotherapeutic cure for malignancy in a human solid tumor.

Because it was an unusual tumor with an immunological component (the placenta being considered tissue the mother's body could reject), that first success was attributed to "spontaneous remission." Nobody would accept it as proof that chemotherapy could cure cancer. Li was asked to leave NIH.

After Roy Hertz admitted that first cancer patient, NCI's scientific director, Bo Mider, recruited Gordon Zubrod, an oncologist with a solid scientific background and excellent administrative skills, to be clinical director for the NCI. As part of the team that had worked on the anti-malarial drug program at Goldwater Memorial in the early days of World War II, Zubrod had learned something about drug development. "When Gordon came in 1954, oncology was one of the lesser disciplines in clinical medicine," says Alan Rabson, NCI's good-humored deputy director. "Clinical medicine was dominated by people who studied the kidney, who measured clearances and had all sorts of data. At the bottom of the barrel of clinical medicine were oncologists, who were known as poison doctors. Gordon played more of a role in changing that image than any other single person."

Zubrod began recruiting a cadre of promising oncologists, two of whom had remarkably similar names: Emil Frei III, whom everyone called Tom, and Emil Freireich, whom everyone called Jay. Frei and Freireich were aware of preclinical studies of combination chemotherapy by Howard Skipper and Abe Goldin. As luck would have it, Jay Freireich had rented a house in Bethesda next door to Lloyd Law, a giant in cancer biology and one of the NIH's first "mouse" doctors. Law and Freireich had adjoining backyards, unseparated by a fence, so they got to know each other. Freireich learned that Law had had some success administering combinations of chemicals ("combination chemo," as it would become known) to leukemic mice.

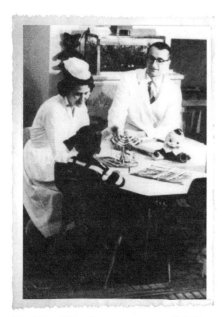

Emil Frei III, whom everyone called Tom, with a nurse and patient

Lloyd told Freireich about his experiments; Freireich told Frei; they consulted with Zubrod, and against strong external resistance from a cancer community that felt the science wasn't ready for it, Frei and Freireich introduced intensive combination chemotherapy for the treatment of acute lymphocytic leukemia of childhood. At the time, a diagnosis of leukemia amounted to a death sentence.

In the early 1960s, surgery and radiotherapy were considered the only appropriate treatments by mainstream cancer researchers, who denounced Frei and Freireich's approach as "toxin of the month." They felt chemotherapy drugs should never be used in combination because they were poisonous and because tumors developed resistance to them. "The dogma was you must treat with single agents one at a time," says Rabson, "and when the tumor became resistant to the first one, you still had the second one, and the third. The concept of mixing them together was thought to be absolute madness." Rabson remembers with amused regret his words at the time, "If you take one ineffective drug and mix it with another ineffective drug, don't expect an effective combination."

It had been shown, however, that combinations of drugs had a synergistic, not just an additive, effect, so there was some reason to think combination chemotherapy would work. Also, Frei and Freireich had strong support from their boss, Gordon Zubrod, who proposed dividing clinical trials with new cancer drugs into three phases. Frei and Freireich administered four different drugs, with non-overlapping toxicity (so you could use them at full dose), which attacked cells at different phases of the cycle.

Frei and Freireich proved the naysayers wrong and produced the first cure by chemotherapy of a childhood cancer. Their achievement helped to establish the intramural Cancer Institute as willing to take high risks for high rewards—based on evidence of a good chance an experiment would work. At first, only a small percentage of the young leukemia patients treated were cured, but the research has continued, and today acute lymphocytic leukemia is curable in 80 percent of children. Now the NCI is testing the long-term effects of radiation therapy given long ago for children with leukemia that had reached the brain (most drugs do not cross the blood-brain barrier).

A young clinical associate named Vincent DeVita would take the lead in similar work on Hodgkin's disease, the first adult cancer of a common organ system to be cured by chemotherapy. And in the multidrug

Emil Freireich, whom everyone called Jay, with a cell separator

therapy trials for Hodgkin's, huge proportions of the patients treated were cured.

Li, Frei, Freireich, and DeVita were asking the question, "Could you ever cure advanced cancer with chemotherapy?" at a time when cancer was believed to be an incurable disease and chemotherapy was regarded by many as the cruel use of toxins in patients already facing certain death. "Tom Frei created the environment where you could ask the question," recalls DeVita, now at the Yale Cancer Center. "No other institution in the world would even dare to ask that kind of a radical question. Between the two diseases, we proved the point that cancer *could* be cured with chemotherapy—something that's been subsequently proven many times over. You had to have a place like the Clinical Center, and you had to have people who were willing to let the unaddressable questions be addressed." The Clinical Center became the center for "proof of principle."

M.C. Li finally did get recognition for his early work in chemotherapy. In 1972, most of the Lasker Awards presented for research on cancer treatment went to researchers in the Clinical Center: Paul P. Carbone, Vincent T. DeVita, Jr., Emil Frei III, Emil J. Freireich, Roy Hertz, James F. Holland, Min Chiu Li, Eugene J. Van Scott, and John L. Ziegler, with a special award to C. Gordon Zubrod. More importantly, these investigators provided invaluable training to many others. Vince DeVita alone trained ninety-three people, a third of whom have gone on to head cancer centers around the country.

Emil Frei III   *Emil Freireich*

A scientific "marriage of convenience"

Charles F. McKhann, who presented the Charles F. Kettering Prize to Emil Frei III and Emil J. Freireich in 1983, described qualities in the two scientists that made their partnership both fruitful and interesting: "One is politically conservative, the other is very liberal; they probably cancel each other out in major elections. One could probably eat a little more, the other is a gourmet cook. One abounds with ideas, both possible and impossible; the other specializes in the possible. One is verbal and volatile, often right but never wrong. The other is quieter, contemplative, and reasoning. One is relaxed and casual in his lifestyle; the other is neat, precise, almost compulsive. Perhaps most important, both firmly attest that they have never, ever, agreed on anything. However different Frei and Freireich may be, each brought to this scientific 'marriage of convenience' a willingness to reason and compromise that allowed them to do a monumental piece of work—to cure childhood leukemia."

Ethical wills were first described in the Hebrew Bible 3,000 years ago, but references to them have been found in Christian and other cultures as well. Initially, they were transmitted orally, evolving over time into written documents. With today's technology, some are videotaped. Many people create ethical wills at turning points in their lives or when facing challenging life situations. These letters or videos often are shared with family and community while the person is still alive. Bettina Brickell was twenty-nine years old when she died. This letter to her family and friends was read at her memorial service. It is the most frequently read ethical will on my website.

—Barry Baines, M.D.

Bettina Brickell's Ethical Will

Dear friends and loved ones,

As I contemplated this memorial service, I felt great gratitude in my heart that each of you would be here to say goodbye to me. Many of you have shared your warmth, kindness, and love with me during these last months. I want to say thank you and goodbye and share with you the lessons I've learned through my dying.

I have profoundly experienced that love is all that matters. Like many people, I occasionally got caught in my pettiness and separation, thinking I knew the right answer. I judged others, and I have judged myself even more harshly. But I have learned that we carry within ourselves the abundant wisdom and love to heal our weary heart and judgmental mind.

During the time of my illness, I have loved more deeply. My heart feels as if it has exploded. I do not carry anger. I feel we are all doing the best we can. Judging others closes the heart, and when one is dying, that is a waste of precious sharing. Life is how we stand in relationship to both ourselves and to others. Loving and helping each other are all that is important.

We are in the fall season. I feel privileged to die as the leaves fall from the trees. There is a naturalness to the cycle of life and death and for whatever reason, it is my time to die, even though I am young. It is okay. It is right and natural. Life is not about how long we live but about how we live, and I have had a good life. I accept my dying as part of the wondrous process of life.

My sadness is in leaving you. I'll miss the deep comfort and love of gently waking up in (my husband) Peter's arms, giving up our dreams of future years together. I'll miss the sunny days of fishing with my dad, of sharing with my mom her love of life and cosmopolitan savoir-faire. I'll miss giggling with my sister Maria over life's impasses. How appreciative I feel when I think of my brother Michael's faith and encouragement of me...

As I lay dying, I think of all of you, each special in your own way, that I have loved and shared this life with. I reluctantly give up walking on this beautiful planet, where every step is a prayer. The glistening sun on the trees, the sound of a brook as it makes its way down the mountain, the serenity and beauty of a gentle snowfall, sitting at the rim of a Utah canyon and catching a glimpse of eternity—these are the things I have loved.

Please do not think I have lost a battle with cancer, for I have won the challenge of life. I have shared unconditional love. I have opened to the mystery of Spirit and feel that divinity is all around us every day and provides us with a path on which our spirit may take flight.

Chief Crazy Horse said upon his final battle, "It is a good day to die because all the things of my life are present." That is how I feel as I think of the abundance, adventure, opportunity, and love in my life.

When you think of me, know that my spirit has taken flight and that I loved you.

With my love, Bettina

Ray Quinn's Ethical Will
12/29/1938 - _____

What I have learned so far on the 'dash'

Dear Michelle, Dan, and my dearest Stephanie,

First of all, I want you to know how important all of you are in my life journey and how much I love you. It was seldom that my full-blooded Irish father said the words, "I love you," but we never doubted it for an instant. I am sorry that you, Michelle (Mik) and Dan (Daniel Patrick Joseph Paul) never knew your Irish Grandpa, but your good humor and hard work carry on his spirit, and the gleam in his eye is there in each of yours. I have tried hard to be a conduit to you from him. Of course, your French Grandpa Turgeon knew you, Michelle. I wish he had known you better, Dan, since you were only two when he died. I am so glad that he permitted this Irishman to marry his only daughter.

Education has been very important to me throughout my life so far. My mother and dad nurtured that love of learning. They taught me that it is not so much degrees or certificates as it is about being better prepared to serve people's needs more efficiently and effectively. I can see that you have both learned that well. Michelle, as I told you before, you are a great mother to Emily and her brother yet to be born (7 aka VII). I'm sure you absorbed much of that mother love and dedication from your mom, who did such a good job as mother to you and Dan. The magic and love that you and Bob have for each other is certainly a huge factor in your parenting. Bob has always been just like a big brother to Dan, and I am so proud that he is part of our family.

Travel has always been a top priority with me. Seeing new places and the amazing variety of God's creations has been a fun ride. I like the challenges of imagining what to do, from camping and biking across Canada to visiting most of the western states. I usually came up with the "great ideas," and you, Stephanie—the practical one—helped us know how to do it. I hope you continue to remember the good times we had and still do. Sometimes it is just a great trip downtown on the light rail or a quick canoe ride, swim, and picnic at Cedar Lake. Those "mini vacations" always replenish my spirit, and my hope is that they will continue to do that for you, too. Sometimes I have found that the short, simple travels are easy and unencumbered.

I am still working hard, and probably will for the rest of my 'dash,' on being able and willing to ask for help. You are always there, Stephanie, and often anticipate most every need of the three of us. In recent times, we have learned the power of the prayer of Jabez, and God has indeed blessed us, enlarged our territory (and our family). I am so glad that God protects and supports us daily.

One last thought from me through the words of Father Mychal Judge, who died in the 9/11 debacle: "Lord, take me where you want me to go, let me meet who you want me to meet, tell me what you want me to say, and keep me out of your way." My hope for you is that you would join me in asking God to bless your days as you live the rest of your 'dash' in the spirit of Mychal's prayer.

I love all of you with all my heart and soul. I pray that all of us continue to have health, happiness, and prosperity and generously contribute to the lives and welfare of those we meet.

Dad(dy) and Lover

After I told this story to a fellow member of the Association of Personal Historians, she reminded me how important it is for a personal historian to follow her own advice and preserve her own personal history. This brief memoir was a first step toward that goal and a way to honor my grandmother, the woman who most influenced my life. Now that I've written about my special memories of Murdee, I'll save these pages and a dried daffodil in a rosewood box as a someday-gift for my infant granddaughter, so she'll remember, too.

—*Paula Stallings Yost*

Daffodil fields

Paula Stallings Yost

Is everyone blessed with a guardian angel, a soul mate, someone to guide her through this life and beyond? Maybe. Maybe not. All I know is that I have been.

From my earliest memories, I've known the warmth and security of a cocoon of love spun by my own special angel—Murdee. I must have felt our deep connection even before I could form words for it. As the story goes, I refused to call her Grandmother or Granny or Nanny. Instead, I insisted on trying to say "Mother" whenever she entered the room. What came out was "Murdee," which my mother's mother accepted as her official name from that day forward and insisted on others using as well.

Mama, a very busy gal, was divorced before my first birthday, and it would be more than a decade before I met my father. So I spent most of my childhood under the watchful, sparkling hazel eyes of my tiny yet larger-than-life grandmother. She filled all the empty spaces. If I needed the comforting arms of a mother, Murdee was there. If I lacked the stern guiding hand of a father, she extended hers without hesitation. Protector, playmate, confidante, teacher—so many roles played so effortlessly. Perhaps my favorite came at bedtime when she became storyteller and songstress.

Wrapped in my grandmother's ample arms atop sun-dried sheets, I would fight sleep and beg for more and more stories about her childhood on an East Texas farm. As the next to youngest of thirteen children, Murdee never ran out of tales of adventure and mischief. My favorite probably was the one about playing hooky from school with her best friend Alfie.

They must have been about ten years old, she told me, and really had nowhere to go and nothing in particular to do. But it was the first day of spring, and they couldn't bear to stay inside that stuffy one-room schoolhouse another minute. When the teacher clanged the bell after lunch, calling the children back to class, the two girls ran in the opposite direction, making their way toward the woods nearby. Under a canopy of sweetgum, hickory nut, and sassafras trees, they braided red clover into tiaras to wear above their pigtails and gathered buckeyes for good luck. Then it was time to go home and 'fess up as to their whereabouts that afternoon.

Slinking along a dirt road turned white with fallen dogwood blooms, Murdee and Alfie began wondering what had come over them to do such a foolish thing. The nearer they drew to home, the more stories they invented, and the more nervous they became. Topping the hill, where they would have to split up and follow separate paths, the chattering girls suddenly were struck speechless. Below them lay a golden field of daffodils. "I swear," said Murdee. "Those daffodils hadn't been there that morning when we walked to school. But there they were—as yeller as the summer sun and goin' on clear to China!"

Without a word, the two raced down the hill headlong into that field. "We jest plopped down and rolled ourselves through those blossoms like there was no tomorrow," Murdee said. "Turned plum yeller, we did."

I don't remember what happened to my grandmother after she finally made it home that day. But I'll never lose that vision of her romp in the daffodils.

Decades later, as Murdee lay dying at the age of ninety-three, that vision kept coming to me. For five days and four nights, my sister Susan and I held vigil at her bedside. Susan had come along almost eighteen years after I was born, but her ties to our grandmother were forged in the same love-steel as mine. Though Murdee no longer could reply, I talked nonstop and convinced myself of her visual responses. I sang her favorite songs, like "Don't sit under the apple tree with anyone else but me" and "I'll be seeing you…in all the old familiar places." I told her favorite stories. I thanked her for the myriad blessings and lessons she had given me.

I gave her permission to die.

"Murdee, I'll be okay. Because of you, I can survive and surmount. I can find joy in a speck of dust. I can find love in my heart in good times and bad. You did your job well; now it's time for us to let go. I know Alfie's waiting for you in that field of daffodils. All I ask is that when you get there, you'll send me a sign. I need to know."

Within a few hours, my lifelong best friend was gone. Her spirit embraced me before leaving as I sat holding her cool hand, my head upon her shoulder.

We buried my grandmother in her beloved East Texas soil beneath a gravestone already ordered and etched with the name Murdee, per her wishes. A cold drizzle was falling on that March morning as we drove from Dallas to the funeral home in the tiny town of Edom, where she had been raised. I was sitting in the back seat of our Suburban, lost in thought, when we turned off the interstate. Suddenly, a blinding beam of light shone through my window. I glanced up. My red, swollen eyes widened as my long-time mental vision became a reality. Just outside my window stood a glorious field of daffodils "as yeller as the summer sun and goin' on clear to China."

I had my sign.

On my grandmother's birthday, a year after her death, I strolled into an art gallery in Palmer, Alaska, and walked straight to a portrait of a woman looking much like Murdee and standing in a field of daffodils. That painting now hangs over my staircase at home.

Recently, I had a bad day. My mother's husband had suffered a stroke, and I had driven more than two hundred miles in a rainstorm and heavy traffic to pick her up in one town and take her to see him in a hospital in another town. Feeling resentful about leaving behind a long overdue writing assignment and less than comfortable about spending time with a mother I barely knew, I grumbled a lot but had no choice. Murdee long ago extracted my promise to "watch after her baby." I suppose she knew nobody else would put up with her daughter's demands. On the road that day, I glanced upward more than once, thinking, *Okay, Murdee, I better be earning points for this one!*

Our visit to my ailing stepfather done, Mother and I were driving back to her house when she said, "You know, I still have Murdee's old silverware. The set with the wild rose pattern, remember?"

"Yes." Of course, I remembered. That wild rose vine rambled down my cereal spoon most every morning of my childhood.

"I was thinking maybe you should have it," she said.

Shocked at this rare offer of generosity, I grew silent. Mama often reneges on promises made in weak moments, especially if the recipient doesn't display just the right reaction. But the first thing she did upon arriving home was to bring out an old wooden box and place it on her dining room table.

I raised the dusty lid and removed a teaspoon from its bed of sapphire velvet. Looking closely, I recognized my latest message from Murdee. The wild rose had disappeared. In its place was a proud, lone daffodil. Without speaking, I laid the spoon in my mother's hand.

"My God," Mama said, sinking into the nearest chair. Never the sentimental sort, she had always pooh-poohed my daffodil theory—until that moment. Now, even she is a believer.

Over the years, many things have changed, but the miracle of Murdee's daffodils has remained constant. I have returned to my native East Texas. Every spring, I look forward to finding random daffodils scattered across my property at the lake. I didn't plant them. Neither did the birds spread the seeds, as so often happens with other flowers. Daffodils grow only from bulbs planted deep in the ground.

When I least expect it, or sometimes most need it, a daffodil is sure to appear in one form or another. And I'll know Murdee is still with me.

A field of daffodils with a guardian angel waiting—the perfect combination for a granddaughter in need

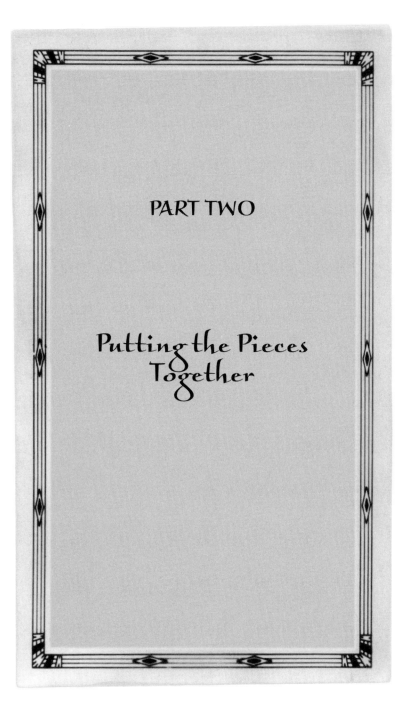

PART TWO

Putting the Pieces
Together

Introduction

There are almost as many ways to create a personal history as there are reasons to do so. The selections in this section illustrate some methods of gathering, organizing, and presenting materials for a personal history.

Like many personal historians, Stephanie Kadel Taras got her start by interviewing members of her family. "The Runaway," based on an interview with her seventy-seven-year-old grandfather, was a story he previously had shared only with his wife. Cynthia Wright's uncle told such fascinating tales of his days as a Moravian missionary in 1930s Alaska that she brought him a hand-held tape recorder and promised to transcribe the tapes if he would record his stories. The resulting four tapes and Cynthia's transcribed stories are family treasures now that her uncle is gone.

Sometimes one person does the research for a personal history, and another puts the material together. Lisa Kagan wrote "The Journey of Henry Kagan," the story of her grandfather's life, based on her uncle's conversations and oral history interviews with his father over the years.

As a sixtieth birthday gift, Linda Blachman audio-recorded the life story of her friend Kathryn Neustadter, including Kathryn's "Life Letter." The intent of life letters, says Linda, is to dig beneath the chronicle of events in a life "to assess the meaning and value of experience and to convey wisdom, wishes, and blessings."

Many journalists become personal historians partly because they enjoy interviewing people and partly because this longer form allows a fuller life story than either print or broadcast journalism typically permits. Working with her client's memories of his mother, and with snippets of an interview his wife had done with her in the 1970s, Andrea Gross rearranged the material for narrative flow in "The Jeweler from America," staying deliberately true to the mother's manner of speaking.

Often, the person being interviewed simply inspires us to take an extra step. Susan Hessel interviewed Courtney Chambers, a young girl with cognitive disabilities, five times for a local television program about kids, and came to admire her tremendously. When Courtney graduated from high school, Susan used software available on the Internet to create a customized book featuring Courtney's story and photos taken over the years.

Sometimes personal histories are collected as part of a larger project. As a volunteer at St. Mary's Center, a non-profit agency that serves low-income and homeless seniors in Oakland, California, Trena Cleland collected the oral histories of twelve of the seniors. Their inspiring stories, told in their words, helped educate the community about St. Mary's work and the elders it serves.

Patrica Kuentz conducted a ninety-minute interview with Ollie Miller for the Veterans History Project, providing both Ollie and the Library of Congress with a recording of his World War II story so future generations could learn of his experiences. As part of the same project, Gillian Hewitt trained a group of aspiring young Canadian writers and historians in the art of oral history interviewing and life-writing. One of her students wrote "Prisoner of War," a story based on her interview with a woman who, as a young child, survived World War II in a prisoner of war camp in the Philippines.

Sometimes illness or advancing age precipitates movement toward recording a personal history with a focus on the illness, the person's life, or both. Linda Blachman founded the nonprofit Mother's Living Stories Project in 1995 to help women with breast cancer who were raising small children. One of those women, Leona Reardon ("Taking Out Emotional Insurance"), wrote letters to her son and made videotapes, "because I wanted him to know what I looked like and what I sounded like." Christine Chamberlain helped Maria Barr produce a narrative ("Finding Maria") about Maria's treatment for breast cancer, her family, her job, and the complexities of juggling them all—drawing both on Maria's journal and on conversations the two women had over the course of a year.

Through conversations, videotaped interviews, and editing sessions, Marc Johnson began helping his mother preserve her life memories before an aggressive cancer struck, which took her life two years later. "Living Life, Learning Lessons" also revealed an interesting moment in American social history.

For those who enjoy writing but feel overwhelmed by the idea of creating a life story, it's often easiest to start with a short piece about a possession that has sentimental value or with a brief but important incident in their lives. Annie Payne ("A Taste of Life") uses her story of a green glass butter dish—a family heirloom—as a visual memory trigger when she speaks about the value of personal histories and encourages people to preserve the history of objects with special meaning to the family.

Sarah White wrote "The Plunge" while leading her first reminiscence writing group, where participants were assigned a common theme for their stories (to help them focus). Sharing life stories aloud in a group can motivate the writer, create powerful bonds, and be healing as well.

Often it's just easier to hire a personal historian to get a project done. Harold Hirshman ("Soup") hired Kitty Axelson-Berry's personal history firm to edit, design, print, and bind his personal memoirs—a book of family stories, personal reflections, and transcribed journals and letters. Douglas Lowe wrote many drafts of his own life story, with the help of personal historian Arlene Campanella, before finding his voice in "Stand Up and Hook Up."

Richard Harding and his son Bob ("Our Secret Code") created an inspiring joint memoir after a traumatic brain injury left Bob a spastic quadriplegic without voice, sight, or muscle control. Rae Jean Sielen's personal history team provided interviewing, writing, and production services that made it possible for Richard (legally blind from macular degeneration) to write and publish their book, *The Rock*, which describes their perseverance and ingenuity in the face of seemingly insurmountable barriers to communication.

If they could do it, you can, too.

My client wanted a book that combined his own memories of his mother, Meta Bejzer, with snippets of a short interview his wife had done with her in the 1970s. This story was excerpted from one of those interviews. While I rearranged Mrs. Bejzer's words for narrative flow, I deliberately stayed true to her manner of speaking, including the way she directly addressed her daughter-in-law.

—Andrea Gross

The Jeweler from America

Meta Bejzer, Narrator

You want to know about when I met Daddy? Let me tell you. Dr. Lifsky lived next door to us in my town, Bereza Kartuska in Poland. One day he came over and said to my mother, "Sarah, I am getting a visitor, an old friend who used to live in Warsaw. Now he has a jewelry store in America. He's a *macher* [Yiddish for big shot] there."

The doctor didn't have to finish what he was saying. My mother knew. "Of course, bring him over," she said. "Our house is your house."

My mother and father liked everybody. Old people, young people... It didn't matter. They were very modern. Usually parents say, "Children, you are not supposed to talk. You have to go to sleep." But not in our home. In our home, there was always talking and singing and dancing. My sister Taiba was our musician. I played the mandolin too, but not as good as Taibala."

"She plays like an angel," Dr. Lifsky always said. "I open my window so I can hear her music." Here in Los Angeles, a neighbor would call the police and say she was making too much noise. But in the Old Country, our neighbor said to my mother, "You are the luckiest woman in the world because there is always music coming from your house.

Meta Bejzer, who left Poland in 1936

The next Sunday, my cousins were over. We were playing games and laughing when the doctor walked in with a very handsome gentleman and said, "This is Mr. Jacob Bejzer."

Mr. Bejzer, your daddy, was dressed like a *macher* all right. He had on a dark blue, three-piece suit and a big hat. And I remember he had a white handkerchief sticking out of his coat pocket.

My mother shooed Taibala off the sofa so the men could sit down. She wanted them to be comfortable. Always she was worried that people should be comfortable. But my father, may he rest in peace, started asking Daddy questions. "Why did you leave home, Mr. Bejzer?" "What kind of family did you come from?"

"Shh, Fischel, shh," said my mother. "Mr. Bejzer doesn't need all these questions. He needs food. Everybody needs food." And she ran into the kitchen. Mama always had fresh mandelbrot [twice-baked almond bread similar to biscotti]. Our house smelled like Canter's [a Jewish bakery and delicatessen in Los Angeles]. On this day, she brought out the mandelbrot, a big bowl of fruit, and tea.

"Mama likes this man," whispered Taibala. She was giggling and eating the cookies at the same time. "She wants you to marry him." Taibala looked at Mr. Bejzer. "You must be a very important man to live in America," she said.

Your daddy turned red in the face. "Not so important," he tried to explain. "Not so important, but too important, I think, to spend my life winding clocks." He made a funny face, and Taibala laughed. Then Mr. Bejzer laughed, too. And I thought how nice he looked when he crinkled his eyes. "My father had a store in Warsaw," he continued. "Forty-seven years in one spot. Every day, I was winding clocks for him. And once a week, I went to the army barracks to wind clocks for them. I was getting a little wound up myself!"

This time everybody laughed, even my mother, and pretty soon I think we forgot what we were laughing about. We were just laughing because we were enjoying each other. Finally, my mother wiped the laugh-tears from her eyes.

"Stop teasing Mr. Bejzer," she said, "or he won't like our house." Then she gave him some more mandelbrot. Poor Daddy. He ate so much mandelbrot that day, I thought he was going to explode.

So that afternoon, there were nine or ten people in our little house, and everybody was laughing and having a good time. Even your daddy took off his suit coat and started to dance.

Daddy stayed in Warsaw for two months. They were good months. Your daddy got a belly. He was skinny when he first came to our house, but soon the dark blue suit became tight.

And then one night right before he was to leave for America, he asked my father if he could talk with him. They went into a small room off the kitchen and shut the door. Taibala grabbed my hand. "Come on," she said. We tiptoed into the kitchen and put our ears to the door, but we could not hear the conversation. Finally, we went back to the living room.

The men weren't in the small room but for a few minutes. When they came out, it had been decided. I was to get married and go to America.

I loved your daddy, but I was so happy in my home. The trouble in Germany was only a shadow. On the one hand, I knew it was there. But on the other, I didn't believe it, even though my brother Avrum had been drafted into the Polish cavalry.

Avrum wrote letters home. Other boys who were drafted used to write letters and say, "Mom, I'm going to die. Get a grave for me because I'm going to die." But not my brother, he would never say things like that. Instead he wrote,

"I'm the richest guy in the world because I have two shoes. But guess what… The shoes both fit on the same foot!" See, he talked about the good things. He saw the bad things, but he made jokes about them. He learned that because he grew up in a happy house.

Now my father said I must leave this house. He sat me down on the sofa. "Metala," he said, "you are my sunshine. I do not want you to go away, but it is hard times in Europe. You will be safe in America. Jacob will be a fine husband." He promised that my whole family would come to America as soon as Avrum got out of the army. "We will see you soon, Metala."

I never… I never saw them again.

The clients of St. Mary's Center, a non-profit agency that serves low-income and homeless seniors in Oakland, California, are scrappy survivors. As a volunteer, I collected the oral histories of twelve of them with an eye to learning what they could teach the rest of us. Their inspiring first-person stories have been widely used to educate the community about this transformative agency and the remarkable elders it serves. In this excerpt from one of those oral histories, Alabama native James Jermany describes how he blossomed with the fellowship of kind staff and friends he made at the center. James's hardscrabble life experiences as an itinerant construction worker, longshoreman, hobo, father of fourteen, alcoholic, and street person had taken their toll on him by the time he found St. Mary's. With the agency's support, he secured safe housing and maintained his sobriety. James died in 2006 at the age of seventy-four, an advocate for the rights of poor people, a loyal volunteer, and a respected member of the community.

—Trena Cleland

Confiscatin' Feelings

James Jermany, Narrator

I used to be as mean as a snake in mating time. You did something wrong to me, I beat you up bad, simple as that. Especially when I was drunk. I'd do anything I could for you. But if you did me wrong, I'd bust you up.

I'm from Alabama. I didn't know my daddy; he was killed when I was two years old. I don't know how. All I know is he was dead. There were seventeen of us brothers and sisters. I was the baby of the family, but I took care of the family's business and everything else. See, my brothers didn't read or write. They didn't have time. They had to be on the farm, so they didn't think about school.

We butchered our animals and had smoked ham, smoked sausage, chitlins, the whole works. Good Southern cookin'… Cakes and pies and collard greens and lima beans and black-eyed peas, ham hocks, pigs' tails and ears, sauce. We grew everything we needed, like corn, beans, greens, potatoes, watermelons, and cantaloupes. We didn't go to town for nothing 'cept the fancy stuff, like cheese. We made our own butter and our own sugar, too.

I started smoking when I was five years old. I played with my older brothers, and you know how older kids are. They introduced me to all their ways.

We left Alabama and went to Pennsylvania when I was five years old. Pennsylvania was steel country. Pennsylvania made me wild.

I tried to be around friends, but you know how kids are. They get together, and if one don't like you, they all not gonna like you. And there was a pack of 'em. So I had to fight with them. I didn't want to fight with them; I wanted to play with them. I didn't want to hurt no one, never. I hurt my hand hitting one in the eye, and owww! So I run from them to keep from fightin' them. When I got tired of running, I started bangin' 'em up. They said I was just crazy or something like that.

When I was eight years old, I made me a pushcart. See, down on the farm, we had no problem. But when we moved to Pennsylvania, it was a whole different thing. I was gonna help my mother get some money. I was out there hustling. Scrap yards and junkyards would buy all the broken glass, bottles, rags, cardboard, and junk I could collect on the streets. After school, I'd get out my little cart. And on weekends, that's all I did.

I stayed in school until I was about sixteen, then I was in the penitentiary. The time in the pen was hard, really hard. People in the penitentiary try to make a woman out of you, and you're a man. I *know* I'm not goin' that way. You'd have to kill me first. We fought in there. I went in there fighting, and prison made a mad dog out of me.

I did five years. I was twenty-one when I came out.

I used to be kind of a rough dude to handle, you know? When I got drunk, I put my war paint on, got my toma-hawk, and went lookin' for some scalps. I didn't care where they come from. You couldn't whisper around me. If you were whispering, and everyone would laugh, I would go over and jump on you. I was Dr. Jekyll and Mr. Hyde, Wolfman, and Frankenstein.

That's changed a whole lot since I came to St. Mary's. They've made me look at aspects of myself. Now, I'm much more calm. If somebody do me wrong, I push it aside.

The staff here, they're all so friendly and always wanting to help. So I confiscated some of those feelings and kept them for myself. I started doing this and doing that, and the more I did, the more better I felt. If I meet someone who needs help, I'm gonna help him. And they like me for that. They like me quite a bit! I feel good, just to know that people care that much for me. They say, "Look what you did for us!" I had never thought of that.

I put that out in front now. I wave it like a banner. I want everybody to see it; I want you to hear it, check it out for yourself. C'mon and get some of this!

I have a hard time breathing because of emphysema and asthma. Asbestos and chemicals… They didn't tell you how dangerous that was on you in the construction business. Plus I had bad sinuses as a kid. I brought them on myself by playing in the snow until I got so cold, my face felt like blocks of wood. Wouldn't wear no hat. And then I smoked cigarettes for fifty years.

I played music. I blew horn, played piano, and danced in nightclubs. Oh, man! I can't blow no horn anymore on account I ain't got no wind. Can't play the piano or organ like I used to play 'cause I broke my hand. Can't dance; I broke my pelvic bone. They say, "If you don't use it, you lose it."

See, when I was small in Alabama, my brothers and sisters would be playin' the guitars. When they got tired and took a break, they'd lay the guitar down on the bed. I'd get down there and play what they played. I could play it by ear. But I was too little, too short, for the organ. I pumped it up with my leg, then sat up on the bench and played, then jumped down and pumped it, then sat up and played. We played blues.

On Fridays, Saturdays, and Sundays, they played music in places, and a lot of people would be dancin' and eatin' fish and fightin' and drinkin' and gettin' drunk. *[laughs]*

My main thing now is trying to get all this evilness out of the street. I talk to young fellas when I see them about this gangland stuff they doing—killin' and all this.

When I was a youngster, I always respected my elders. If you're an older man or woman than me and you tell me something, I say, "Yes, ma'am," and I'm gone. I'm going to do what you say. If I'm doing something wrong, I stop. I won't let you see me doin' it no more.

But see, a lot of these kids you can't speak to now. They call you nasty names. So I don't bother because I could still get violent. Ohhh, just like that. I do bodily harm, too. I'm little, so I gotta work fast! *[laughs]* But I would have to be pushed something terrible for it to happen. Like if they hit me or something, I might come off then. But talkin' ain't nothing. St. Mary's taught me not to be violent. It's growin' on me, nonviolence!

This recovery group we have at St. Mary's is a combination of drug addicts, alcoholics, and people that's got pressure on 'em from different things goin' on in life. We tell them, "Hey, we accept you. People make mistakes. We're not goin' to chase you away because you went out and got on your bender last weekend. Just get a grip on yourself and come back Monday. Eventually, you'll quit."

And they do quit. Then they're so glad, and they're proud they found a place like this. And I'm proud to be a member of it. That's right.

I'm involved in helping out in the drop-in center, political advocacy, all kinds of things. We're always trying to help somebody. St. Mary's has so many programs going, I can't do 'em all. *[laughs]* I make the ones I can.

I'm still growing, still getting better. I find I can leave more and more derogatory stuff alone. At night, I sleep in peace; get up in the morning and feel good and rested.

James Jermany

During my three-year recovery from a disabling back injury, I wondered what services and resources were available for mothers struggling with far worse situations: women living with cancer while raising children. I was shocked to find that they were an underserved, invisible group. As a writer with a long career in public health and counseling, I knew that it would be healing for ill mothers to tell their stories and that the recorded legacies would become invaluable gifts to their children and loved ones if a mother died.

In 1995, I founded the nonprofit Mothers' Living Stories Project. Although I was a trained oral historian and had two decades of interviewing experience, I knew I needed a teacher for working with the ill and dying. I found her in one of the project's support groups. "Taking Out Emotional Insurance" is adapted from Leona Reardon's interview, which appears in Another Morning: Voices of Truth and Hope from Mothers with Cancer (Seal Press, 2006), a book I wrote to bring the mothers' hard-won wisdom and the healing power of story to a wide audience.

—Linda Blachman

Taking Out Emotional Insurance

Linda Blachman

No one wants to get sick. No one wants to think about dying. Perhaps that's why 50 to 70 percent of Americans haven't prepared wills, ensuring that their survivors will inherit a mess. Perhaps that's why most of us still associate the idea of recording histories and legacies with the very ill or very old.

As a healthy, middle-aged parent, I used to think that way, too. Until 1995, when a serious back injury forced me to slow down and revise my life. Until I met Leona Reardon, wise beyond her forty-four years, just as I was founding the Mothers' Living Stories Project to record the life stories of women like her—mothers living with cancer while raising children.

Leona didn't need me to record her story. Unlike most people who want to preserve their personal history but find it too hard to do alone, she had done it all. She had created a book to help her three-year-old son, Gabriel, talk about her illness, as well as videotapes, audiotapes, and letters to prepare him and other loved ones for her impending death from colon cancer. Leona told me she'd be happy to describe what she had done and why it's important for everyone to do. But, she added, "You'd better come soon."

When we met a week later, I asked Leona why she would be willing to grant an interview. Eyes shining, voice clear and composed, her answer was simple: "I've had a good life."

Leona

I feel that I have had a fabulous life. The only thing I haven't done is as much community service as I would have liked. This interview is a way for me to address that. I wish the Project's help with recording my story had been available to me when I first got sick.

What impelled you to begin recording stories for Gabriel?

It started because as a parent, the only thing you can do is prepare your child for life, and if they screw it up, they screw it up, and it's not your fault. But you have to do your best to prepare them for the real world, however you interpret that. So, when I realized that it was likely that I was going to die soon, I started working hard on ways to prepare Gabriel for life without me. I felt that was my obligation as a parent—to make death normal.

I have always written Gabriel letters because I was forty when he was born, and I thought the chances were pretty high that I could die before he thinks to ask questions that I now ask my parents. When I was diagnosed, I realized that writing letters wasn't enough and that I needed to start thinking about conversations that I wasn't going to be able to have with him.

One of the things I thought right away was, *Geez, he's so young, he's not going to remember me.* I borrowed a camera and made videotapes because I wanted him to know what I looked like and what I sounded like. I didn't have a plan, but I had things I wanted to talk about. I wanted to give him a history of my life because I've had a fabulous and interesting life. I was born in Africa, grew up at the end of the British Empire, and saw the British Empire disintegrate.

It was real to me; it wasn't a piece of history. War was something I wanted to talk to him about. When you have a son, you think about that. I do, anyway.

I realized that I was making tapes about issues that were important to *me*. I had made tapes about a lot of adult subject matter, but I wasn't going to be around when he was a teenager, and that's a really difficult time, and I wanted to talk to him about that. And I hadn't done anything for him *now*. So I started reading stories on audiotape to him so that he can have my voice. I started with stories that he likes now as a three-year-old.

We've done some videotaping together. He's seen those, and he'll have those. I have written him letters for life-cycle events I thought would be times when he would miss me. Because I think that children are really resilient, but they get to their wedding or graduation, and the grief recurs. "Oh, God, I wish Mom could have seen the baby or met my wife." So I wrote one for his bar mitzvah and bought him a present. I bought him a tallis (prayer shawl) because I couldn't think of anything else that wouldn't be totally out of date by the time, that wouldn't embarrass him half to death.

I wanted to write to him about who I think he is and what I think is important. He's incredibly bright, but college is not as important to me as who he is. I care whether he's kind and compassionate and self-supporting.

Recently, I told a woman that I used to work with that I had done these things, and she said, "What an interesting process to write to him at these ages when you have no idea who he will be. But how wonderful because in those letters, you are revealing yourself to him in different ways." It was a nice way to put it.

I started because of Gabriel, but it has opened up an incredible dialogue with my family and with people I worked with and at the synagogue. I realized I needed to talk to my family about things for Gabriel, and then I realized that I just needed to talk to my family, especially because my family doesn't want to talk about it.

I wrote and sent the same letter to my family. Then, I wrote a letter to each of them individually about what they've meant to me. I was going to leave those letters with Claire to give to them, and I realized that one of the things that happens when people can't talk about this stuff is they don't get to finish their process. So, I have sent the letters to my family and said, "If you have things you want to talk to me about, now's the time."

I've met many people, ill or well, who believe preparing a legacy will hasten death. It sounds as if you haven't engaged in magical thinking.

Well, Gabriel does that for us; he's very good at that. [*Laughs*] I understand that feeling 'cause when I was diagnosed, I really did think, "I am going to die." And I kept thinking, "Oh, boy, you mustn't think that way because if you think that way, you *will*." Eventually, I came to, "Okay, if I don't die and I do an ethical will or whatever, what's the worst that can happen? I'll have an ethical will—terrific. If I do die, I'll be prepared, and I won't have this anxiety to cope with on top of everything else."

Most people can't do this alone, but they can do it. I say to people, "Okay, so if you don't do this and you don't die, no big deal. But if you don't do this and you die . . . whew." Everyone who can gets health insurance. They don't *not* get health insurance because they might not get sick. It seems like the same thing.

And what has it been like for you to do all this preparation?

It was very exhausting, but it's also incredibly rewarding. I feel like I have had a much more conscious process than I would have had otherwise. I feel like I really will be present in significant events in Gabriel's life, whether he wants me there or not! The other wonderful thing is that I have gotten to say to my teenager all of the things I wanted to say without being interrupted and without having to listen to the back-chat. It's been very healing to do, and it's given me a greater sense of control. It's a way of integrating the concept of death into life. Everyone's going to die, we may as well be prepared. Lots of people don't get to say goodbye, and I have, and I feel incredibly blessed. I have done as much as I can do to make this an okay experience for my child.

Because of Leona Reardon, I have prepared a will, audio-recorded my life story, and written a legacy letter, which I update annually. When I work with private clients of all ages and states of health, I know that I have "walked my talk." Most important, I have told my daughter, who asked me to record my story, that it's done. When I presented her with the archival box on her twenty-first birthday, she joked with age-appropriate dismissal, "Thanks, Mom. Now put it away." The box sits on a shelf with my other insurance files. It will be there when she needs it.

About the time I started conducting interviews as a volunteer for the Library of Congress Veterans History Project, I ran into a former coworker, Renee Miller, who told me that her father-in-law, Oliver Miller, was a veteran with a great story. She introduced me to Ollie, and I interviewed him for ninety minutes. He was thrilled to have his World War II story preserved at the Library of Congress, so future generations could access it and understand more about his experiences. Two years later, Ollie asked me to help write his and his deceased wife's life stories. The following is an excerpt from his book, The Life and Times of Carol and Ollie Miller.

—Patricia A. Kuentz

We Won?

Oliver W. "Ollie" Miller, Narrator

During World War II, I was a map-maker with the G-2 Section in the Office of the Chief of Staff, Division Headquarters, 20th Armored Division in the European Theater. The G-2 Section was a military intelligence group. In fact, we always said that we had so much radio equipment we could probably have contacted SHAEF, the Supreme Headquarters Allied Expeditionary Force in England, if we'd had to. Fortunately for me, our group's role generally kept us behind the front, just in back of harm's way.

Because of our typical location, I was really terrified only a couple of times during the war. The last time was in Germany. Our unit had just arrived in a ski resort area called Tettenhausen, near Salzburg. We knew the war was winding down, as not much military action was occurring by then. Two of my buddies, Furedy and Knetzger, and I decided to drive down and relax on the sunny side of a grassy hill nearby. From a little town below, a narrow dirt road wormed its way up the side of the long hill. We found ourselves a good spot and lay down on our stomachs to enjoy the warm day.

We'd come to the area in a half-track [armored vehicle], and it was sitting right next to us. All of a sudden, one of the guys said, "Look... Look! Look at there! Jesus!" He was pointing to three or four soldiers, Germans we thought, slowly making their way up the hill. We ran over to the half-track and grabbed our rifles. Panicked, we looked

Ollie Miller in his uniform, circa 1945

around for more ammunition but quickly realized that none of us had any more than what was in our rifles.

As the men came closer, we could tell for sure they had on German uniforms. They could see us but didn't appear to be frightened at all, while we were standing there holding our carbines, scared to death and shaking like crazy. We had rarely seen live German soldiers.

Finally, Knetzger said, "Let's stop them and see if we can talk to them." (Knetzger could speak pretty good German and often served as a translator for our group.) After talking with the soldiers a couple of minutes, he turned to us and said, "This guy tells me they've got their discharge papers from the German Army." Knetzger had the Germans take out their papers, and he looked them over. "Yeah, they're discharge papers. They say the war is over!"

Actually, the war **was** over. It hadn't been over long, maybe just a couple of days. Somebody in our group must have known, but we sure hadn't heard.

The three of us were so excited by the news that we ran down to the little town and knocked on the door of the biggest house there. I could see lots of little kids running around in the house. It was some kind of a school for very young children, like a kindergarten. The guy who ran the school didn't know the war was over either. When we told him, he started crying, and then his wife started crying. Before long, everyone was crying. It was wonderful news for those Germans.

We were happy, too. Very happy! But we always wondered how those German soldiers came to know about the war's end before we did. The irony of that situation still resonates with me to this day.

Prisoner of War

Jenny Templer Kyle, Narrator

The year was 1941 when I went into the prisoner of war camp. I was imprisoned, along with my mother, brother, and sister, on the campus of the University of Santo Tomas in Manila, the capital city of the Philippines. The Catholic campus had been converted into an internment camp. It was surrounded by barbed wire. But I was only three years old, so I don't have many memories from that time.

Two years later, in 1943, the camp was becoming too crowded. We were taken 35 miles south to a place called Los Baños. It was also surrounded by barbed wire, and this is where my memories begin.

They put us in barracks. I remember being very jealous of my brother because he was eight years old, and we were in barrack number eight—the second room from the entrance. We lived in one and a half rooms in a barrack made of thin bamboo with a roof of palm fronds. A bare light bulb hung from the ceiling. The floor was dirt. Bunk beds for my brother and my mother were located on one side, and for my sister and me on the other. It was very small, about 8 feet long by 5 feet wide. There were two shelves for our belongings, but we only had two suitcases. That was all we were able to carry.

Life was pretty hard at Los Baños. The worst thing about being a prisoner of war was that there was hardly any food. We had our daily rations of rice, but they always dwindled. Some people had been able to bring cats and dogs into the camp, but they disappeared very soon as people began to eat them. We would go around to the back of the Japanese kitchen and eat their scraps. We got the potato peelings while the Japanese ate the potatoes. We also scrounged lily leaves and very slimy, greasy spinach that grew in that part of the world. At roll call every morning, we would have to stand in rows and be counted. Sometimes the Japanese kept us for a very long time, and the women and the civilian men would chat amongst themselves. The women used to swap recipes. I would hear my mother talking about eggs and cream and butter and things I had never heard of or seen.

Schools were formed in this camp because many teachers, nuns, priests, and missionaries were there. My brother and sister went to school, but I was too young. My mother taught me the alphabet using various things she could see around the camp. For instance, we got one Red Cross parcel during the whole three years we were interned in the camp. My mother put the box on a shelf in our little room and pointed at the letters on its side: *This parcel is a gift from the Red Cross of Canada.* That was my first connection with Canada.

The package was full of wonderful things—Klim (powdered milk), cigarettes to curb your appetite, Spam (canned meat), and all kinds of other things. There was also a pair of children's pink underpants. My sister said, "They're mine"

I said, "No, they're mine!"

Our mother solved the dispute. "Hazel will wear them on Monday, and Jenny can wear them on Tuesday."

Hazel wore them the next Monday. Out she went between the barracks to play in the ditches that would carry off the monsoon rains. Down came the rains in such a flood that they swept the panties right off her. I never got to wear them. Even now when I see my sister, I say, "You owe me a pair of pink underpants."

Whilst my brother and sister were at school, we little ones went around roving in gangs, tormenting the guards when our mothers weren't watching us. When you met the guards, as a sign of respect, you had to bow from the waist with your hands to your sides and your legs straight. We would go up to them, and they would bow, and we would bow. As they walked along, we would run in front of them and bow to them again so they had to bow back. We would repeat this several times until they got sick of it.

After three years, our rations were down to half a cup of rice per person per day. My mother wondered whether she should share her rice with us or keep herself strong in order to deal with us. My brother, who was now eight or nine and growing, tried not to ask for her share. He often left the room and went outside because he was so hungry.

We finally got past Christmas of 1944. Two men in our camp spoke Japanese, but they didn't let on that they did. While eavesdropping on the Japanese, they heard them planning our massacre. The Japanese soldiers were needed in the north of the Philippines to fight the Americans, so they could not man the camp anymore. Their plan was to lob grenades amongst us during roll call on February 22. We would all panic and run to the open gates of the camp and be shot as escaping prisoners of war.

The two men went right to the American head of the camp and asked what to do with this information. He said they should escape and try to get the Americans to come rescue us by February 22. The men slipped out of the camp under the wire and went north. Assisted by the Filipinos, they reached the American troops.

At 7:00 a.m. on February 22, 1945, we went out for roll call. We were standing there when suddenly all these planes came over. I remember looking up and seeing things drop out of the planes. Mother grabbed our hands, rushed us back to our barracks, and shoved us under the bed. I remember saying, "It's not fair. I want to see, I want to see!" Bullets were flying through the walls and pinging off them above us. Mother was desperate to keep us under the bed so we would not be hit.

Finally, the shooting stopped. One group of Americans had come down by parachute and another group crossed the lake on amphibious tractors. The Filipinos had surrounded our camp.

We were told to pack one suitcase per family and were taken to a camp on the other side of the lake. The American soldiers put us up on their shoulders. It was a thrill a minute. Running, having a bar of chocolate, throwing it up because our stomachs couldn't take it. Getting chewing gum all wound round in our hair because we didn't know what chewing gum was...

Finally, it was time to go back into Manila. We were issued Red Cross clothing and food and then put on a ship to Los Angeles. In Los Angeles, we were all put in a camp and treated very well. We even were allowed to go to a department store, where each child could choose a present. My sister chose a doll, which she called Lucy. My brother and I chose holsters. We stayed in California for three more weeks, until we were put on a train to Halifax. Then we waited for a convoy to take us back across the Atlantic to Liverpool.

My grandmother hadn't even heard if we were alive. When we arrived in England, she was horrified at us. We didn't know how to sit in a chair because we had only ever squatted, native-fashion, on the floor. When she gave us food, we put our fingers around it and then sucked our fingers to get the last morsel of food. And, of course, we swore. We had all those wonderful words we had learned through the walls of our camp. She couldn't imagine what we had been through to be like that.

My father spent four years as a prisoner of war in Hong Kong. After the dropping of the atomic bomb, he was liberated and came to England through New York. I can remember my mother getting all excited because Dad was coming home. We were all standing there when he walked down the driveway.

"Your dad's coming," she said.

I hid behind her and peeked out, thinking, *Who is this man?* He must have felt the same thing.

*Hazel, James, and Jenny Templer (left to right) in
Ilfracombe, Devonshire, England, circa 1947*

My maternal grandfather, John Reynolds, the ninth of twelve children, grew up in Martinsburg, West Virginia, where his father was a woolen mill supervisor. John started working—selling candy bars to the mill workers—at the age of five. During a life history interview in 2000, when he was seventy-seven years old, he told me the following story about an incident that occurred when he was a newspaper delivery boy. No one besides my grandmother had ever heard the story before.

—Stephanie Kadel Taras

The Runaway

John Reynolds, Narrator

When I was ten or eleven, I ran away. I thought I was adopted because my parents wouldn't give me any attention or something. I made all the arrangements for my papers to be picked up and so forth. And I was running away with this other kid; I forget his name. We were gonna head south, go to Florida, even back then. My mother had a charge account at the grocery store, and that boy and I were trying to figure out what we could pack to eat so we wouldn't get hungry. Back in those days, maybe 1933, everything was sold in big lots. Finally, we charged a five-pound box of crackers and twenty-five chewing-gum balls to my mother's account.

We hitchhiked right down the Shenandoah Valley on old U.S. 11, traveling by horse and buggy, cars, and everything. A traveling salesman picked us up finally; he was going into Harrisonburg, Virginia. He was listening to the radio, and "The Shadow" came on. You know, you'd hear that squeaky noise and then "The Shadowww knowwws..." And it was just getting dark outside. That program scared the daylights out of both of us.

The salesman parked up on the hill above Harrisonburg and said, "This is as far as I go." We were almost a hundred miles away from home—quite a ways for two young boys. We got out of the car, but the sky was getting darker and darker. This was around the time when the Lindbergh baby

John Reynolds, age eight (far left, second row) and his brother,
Jimmy (far right), with family, circa 1931

got kidnapped, so that was in our minds, too. We went
down to the bottom of the hill and told a policeman there
that we'd been kidnapped. He called our folks in
Martinsburg. They put us up at the Salvation Army that
night and then put us on the bus back to Martinsburg the
next day.

The bus station in Martinsburg was just around the corner from the paper office. Pop met us at the station, and my
bicycle was there. He says to me, "Take your bicycle and go
deliver your papers." So I did.

I got home at suppertime and was greeted with an
absolute blackball. They blackballed me! The whole family

wouldn't speak to me. This was my father's doing. I'm telling you, no one spoke to me.

But that night in bed (I was sleeping with Jimmy then), my brother couldn't hold back anymore. "Where'd you go?" he asked. "Was it hot?"

Oh boy, somebody was finally paying attention to me! I said, "Oh, man, it was hot down there. Really hot!" Of course, Harrisonburg was only a hundred miles down the valley, but I told Jimmy that anyway.

And that's all I remember about it. My parents never discussed it. No one ever discussed it at all. *Until now*.

Thorleif Harberg, my uncle, always told the most interesting stories of his days as a Moravian missionary in Alaska in the 1930s. For years, the family encouraged him to record his stories. He began writing them out but found this a daunting task. In 1997, we visited Uncle Thor and his wife, Elsie, in Florida. I brought him a hand-held cassette recorder and promised that if he would record his stories, I would transcribe the tapes for him. A year later, I received four tapes in the mail. His book is a family treasure today, and his stories will live forever. And now that he has passed, his voice recording is priceless.

—Cynthia Wright

Black Joe

Thorleif Harberg, Narrator

On one of our trips from Bethel, Alaska, I was returning home alone by sled and dog team. I had no real difficulty except for one scary occurrence, which had an interesting conclusion. The trail had been easy, the load was light, so we were making good time. I came to the Ilkivik River when the tide was very low. The Ilkivik is a wide tidewater slough, perhaps three hundred or more feet across at the point where my team and I were to cross.

Strange things happen when tidewater comes in a river. Along each of its banks, the ice is frozen securely into the muddy bottom. This is called anchor ice. When the tide comes in, it raises the ice in the center of the river, leaving the shore ice (anchor ice) underwater since the ice cannot rise with the tide. A traveler simply cannot cross at this stage of the tide. He must wait until the tide recedes and there is no open water. Even then, he must be certain that the new ice caused by the freezing of the water is safe enough to travel across. Delays for a number of hours are common under such circumstances.

I had experienced the dogs getting across such new ice and my falling into the salty water at twenty-five degrees below zero. At that temperature, one freezes quickly. I had to get out my sleeping bag, jump into it, take off my mukluks, socks, and even my long underwear, and change everything while protected from freezing inside the sleeping bag. That was not my problem now.

With the tide out, the anchor ice was evident, but I faced another obstacle. The center ice was too wide for the river when the tide went out. Therefore, it had split in the middle all up and down the center of this 300-foot span between the two shores. The center ice was high and steep. My sled was 14 feet long, and I had a time reaching the front of the sled when I stood on top of the ice. If you can visualize a large, wide W, you can imagine what I was up against. The two sides are the anchor ice, frozen in the mud, with the center like an inverted V.

I had no trouble getting my nine dogs and the sled down the anchor ice, but then I was stuck. With the help of my ice pick, I made my way up to the top of the center ice, which was many feet thick. Where it split on top, the ice broke in a jagged, broken line, leaving lots of air holes or crevasses.

Before ascending the ice, I had put a rope onto my lead dog, Black Joe. I now used it to pull him up to me, and then two dogs at a time. Such scratching for footing I had never seen. I had never done this before. I eased the team down over the other side and began pulling up the 14-foot sled. The load was negligible, and with the help of the dogs, I managed to get it up and balance it on top while I tied the rope to the back of the sled to ease it down the other side. I figured I could then easily slide down on my seat while holding onto the rope so the dogs and the sled would not get away from me.

Once the sled was down, the dogs started moving downriver. I reached for my ice pick, and the ropes snapped from my hand. In my effort to hurry, I stepped into a crevasse that was just big enough for my foot. I was stuck, with one foot caught up to my knee in this crack in the ice. The ice pick was put to work, and after some frantic ice-picking, I got my foot loose.

I looked for my team and saw them heading around the bend in the river, leaving me stranded and not knowing where the next habitation was.

Many things raced through my mind. Am I going to freeze to death out here on the tundra? My sleeping bag was on the sled going away from me. If I follow the riverbank, could I possibly come across an uninhabited, dirt igloo that was used by hunters or trappers? I prayed for protection and for guidance in making the right choices.

Finally, I checked my ankle and found that it was okay, so I slid down the ice and began walking in the direction my team had gone. I had not traveled very far when, to my amazement, I saw my team returning. With joy and thanksgiving, I greeted them, patted each dog, and gave Black Joe special praise for returning.

The tide was beginning to come in the river, and the ice was rising, so I called on the team to head for shore, where we had some difficulty getting over the steep anchor ice to the top of the bank. Once there, I got my compass reading and headed for home.

It would be dark before we reached the village, so I followed the shoreline. This route was a bit longer, but absolutely certain to get me to Kwigillingok. That night, the moon came out full. It was beautiful. The air was crisp and cold, but warm enough that I took off my parka and ran with the sled. A pair of coveralls over all my other wool clothing protected me. The sky was clear, and Black Joe must have known where he was going because he set a fast pace.

Elsie was surprised to see me arrive at 9:00 p.m. I unhitched the dogs, put them in their own shelters, fed and watered them, and then finally went in to share with the family what had happened.

I was with a group of men from the village the next day when I had my translator, Joe, relate my experience of being stranded on the ice and then the team returning for me. As Joe was translating, I saw some of the men smile and look at each other knowingly. I soon learned why. Black Joe had belonged to Wood River Chris, an old sourdough squaw man. His daughter Christina had sold me part of her father's team in 1938 when we arrived in Kwigillingok. The men from the village told me the following true story:

Wood River was quite a drinker. Many times, he would leave the village far from sober. In his drunken condition, he would often fall off the sled and be too drunk to get up and go after his team. He had trained Black Joe to look back every once in a while to see if he was still on the sled. If Wood River wasn't there, Black Joe would lead the team around and back up the trail until he came to where his master lay in the snow. The lead dog would lick and paw Wood River until he got up and staggered back onto the sled. Then he would turn the team towards home again.

My life had been saved because a former master had trained his lead dog to save his life. I thank God for Wood River Chris and Black Joe.

*Moravian missionaries Elsie and Thorlief Harberg
in Kwigillingok, Alaska, circa 1938*

The Journey of Henry Kagan

Lisa Kagan

The story of my grandfather's life begins in the town of Mykolaiv on the Black Sea, where he was born in 1917. Mykolaiv was part of Russia then, but is now part of the Ukraine. My great-grandfather, Joseph Kaganofski, lived there with his wife, Diana, and young son, Henry. Joseph was a Jewish craftsman who supported his family by working as a harness maker for the Tsar. He was paid in small nuggets of gold.

Across Russia, however, the influence of Marxist-Leninist atheism, propaganda, and pressures for modernization and secularization was rapidly gaining strength. Persecution of the Jews was rising. Joseph's shop was taken over by the Bolsheviks—members of Vladimir Lenin's radical wing of the Russian Social Democratic Labor Party. Joseph was demoted from craftsman to cook. Through the frigid winters, he prepared meals for throngs of Russian soldiers.

The Kaganofski family prepared to escape to freedom. They sewed Joseph's remaining gold nuggets into their clothes and pieces of leather. Leaving behind the only life they had ever known, they sought a safe and just place to start again. Their journey began on foot as they climbed a steep hill with their horse beside them. At the crest of the hill, they stopped and looked back at their hometown. Joseph instructed Henry to give the horse to the townspeople. Their starving neighbors were exceedingly grateful, butchering the horse and cooking it on the slope of the hill.

The family followed the path of the Christian Underground Railroad—a series of homes where Christians welcomed migrating Jews and helped them escape. During the day, the Kaganofskis hid in twenty-foot haystacks in the fields. Russian soldiers, searching for Jews, sometimes came and stuck pitchforks in the haystacks. Yet the Kaganofskis survived. By cover of night, they would trudge on to the next hiding station. Joseph, Diana, and Henry were hiding under a trapdoor, beneath a rug and a kitchen table, one cold night when Russian soldiers entered the house and asked the old farmer, "Do you have any Jews here?" As the farmer was telling the soldiers there were no Jews in the house, six-year-old Henry started to sneeze. Diana covered his mouth. Finally, the soldiers left, and the family remained undiscovered.

In Bremerhaven, Germany, the family boarded a steamship headed for America. As the *Bremerhaven* pulled away from the dock, some voyagers held out small balls of yarn, one end of which had been left with relatives or friends on shore. The yarn unwound and eventually ran out, streaming forlornly in the wind.

On the long, arduous journey across the Atlantic, Diana and Joseph struggled to protect themselves and little Henry from hunger and sickness. They anxiously awaited their new life, opportunity, and freedom in America.

The Kaganofskis arrived in New York Harbor and saw the lights of the Statue of Liberty shining through the night mist. They kissed the deck of the boat, crying and thanking God that they had arrived safely.

The *Bremerhaven* docked at Ellis Island. Nervous at the prospect of the various tests required for admittance into this new land, the excited young family stepped onto American soil. Diana was parted from Joseph and Henry as the men and women were sent to separate areas to be deloused by a drenching with a strong antiseptic. After a series of medical tests, the three were declared healthy. Then it was time to register. When a man asked his name, Joseph replied in Russian that it was Kaganofski. Such a long name would not do in America, said the man, shortening it to Kagan.

Upon completion of their screening and registration on Ellis Island, the *Kagans* met with their sponsor, Henry's paternal grandfather. He was a man of biblical proportions with a long, black beard, affectionately called Rasputin because of his physical resemblance to the Russian monk Rasputin, who treated the son of Tsar Nicholas for hemophilia and came to dominate the royal family.

Windows into the life and work of Henry Kagan

Grandfather Rasputin introduced Joseph, Diana, and Henry to the strong Jewish community in Manhattan. They became involved with a Koschovita—a fraternity of Jewish people in which Judaism and prayer united the immigrants. They communicated in Russian and Yiddish until, gradually, they learned English. The East Side below 14th Street supposedly resembled "Jerusalem in its palmist days." The Kagans not only found a strong, welcoming Jewish community that practiced its religion openly; they also were immediately integrated into the neighborhood business district.

Joseph set up a buggy upholstery shop in the Lower East Side of Manhattan with the help of Grandfather Rasputin, proudly displaying a sign in Hebrew. Right away, Joseph put

Henry to work. In addition to the long hours spent working for his father each evening, Henry had to walk three miles to and from school every day. When the buggy shop evolved into a gas station and auto-repair shop, Henry's responsibilities grew. Each night until one o'clock in the morning, he stood on a crate and hand-cranked gas into a hundred or so A&P grocery trucks—trucks with hard rubber tires and wooden spoke wheels. Henry was also expected to wax and polish six to eight Packard cars a day. Meanwhile, Joseph would be upstairs playing cards and smoking with his friends. He never paid his son for his work.

Eventually, this schedule took its toll. Henry dropped out of school before completing the eighth grade. He soon got a job as a milkman in addition to working for his father. Starting at four-thirty each morning, he would drive a horse-drawn milk wagon from apartment to apartment and run up and down countless flights of stairs, delivering bottles of milk. After his return from World War II years later, Henry moved to Long Island, where he worked for Evan's Dairy and even delivered milk to Theodore Roosevelt at Sagamore Hill.

Henry met his wife, Bella Lipschitz, on a blind date. They married soon after and had three children—Lenny, Bruce, and Neil (my father). Eventually, Henry started his own upholstery shop, Pioneer Auto Seat Covers, on Long Island. Though it was a family-owned, family-run business like his father's, Henry believed in paying his children for their labor.

A religious man, Henry led prayers every morning in the Orthodox Jewish community. Yet he worked Saturdays, the Jewish Sabbath, to keep his business going. He believed that hard work and a good job were the keys to security, and that money equaled freedom. He passed these views on to his children. Because of Henry's strong work ethic, his family affectionately referred to him as "The Rock." He also harbored a strong love for America, yet he preserved the important family traditions from the Old World. Henry Kagan maintained a deep sense of inner balance and was very at ease in his life.

Diana, Joseph, and Henry's names are engraved on plaques on the Wall of Honor at Ellis Island. Their children and grandchildren continue to realize their dreams of freedom and prosperity in America, while honoring the struggle that made it all possible.

Douglas Lowe worked with me for more than a year compiling his life stories. After numerous drafts, he continued to believe something more was needed. Following a lot of discussion and personal reflection, he penned this introduction to his manuscript in 2006. As he reflected on his paratrooper training experiences, he managed to crystallize his life within this statement. Here he found his voice, which then resonated throughout his memoir.

—Arlene Campanella

Stand Up and Hook Up

Douglas D. Lowe, Narrator

"Stand up and hook up!"

The jumpmaster's commanding voice, heard over the roar of the C-47 engines, brings twenty jumpers to their feet. *Oh, my God…what am I doing here? Can I really do this?* I'm very nervous, perhaps better described as scared as hell. But we've been through weeks of brutal training to get here, and those of us who made it this far respond to his orders without hesitation.

Facing us, the jumpmaster stands at the rear of the plane beside an open door. Occasionally, as he sticks his head out the door, the force of the wind pulls the skin back on his face so it looks like a skeleton. He is there to give the **'GO!'** order and then make sure we don't freeze in the doorway.

A red light is flashing beside this door. When it changes to green, I'm out the door for my first parachute jump. On this 22nd day of May 1952, we are flying above Fort Benning, Georgia. *How can I look down 1,200 feet and jump out that door?* The adrenaline is flowing strong. *Am I hooked up okay? Will my chute open? Why did I volunteer for this? Wish I could hug my dog Buster once more.* I was told your first jump is the easiest because you don't know what to expect. I think the guy who told me that is nuts!

Suddenly… Green light… **GO!**

As I move forward and out the door, many thoughts of my life are flashing through my mind. A profound jerk brings me back to reality. I look up, and my chute is open.

What a beautiful sight! Curiously, it's now deathly quiet up here, like we are frozen in time. We yell to each other during descent. I tense up for the landing but remember just in time to relax.

I hit the ground, roll to one side as trained, no problem. *Man, this is fantastic!* As the other paratroopers and I collapse our chutes and carry them off the drop zone, we relate our experiences, seemingly all talking at the same time. I am ecstatic. Why didn't I find this thrilling experience before? I can't wait to make four more jumps in the next four days and receive my silver parachute wings.

My life is changing rapidly. I've been away from home almost a year and am now in a new world. At the age of twenty, I have reached a major turning point in my life. Everything is new, exciting, different, and challenging. My first twenty years seem so insignificant, as if they took place eons ago and mean nothing to me.

That youthful focus on myself was wrong. For it was those early years of the good and not-so-good traits, along with the sacrifices and examples from others, that shaped my life. Family commitment, hard work, and responsibility formed the foundation of how I perceived the world. Although at times I may have failed to achieve these ideals, the basics remained with me and helped provide a correction when I deviated from them. New experiences, lessons learned from life's challenges, and the wisdom gained from greater maturity help me reflect on where I've been and where I'm heading in life.

Now as I relate my memoirs, it is my desire that my descendents will learn from the good and not-so-good decisions made in my life and benefit from the lessons I've learned.

Douglas D. Lowe, circa 2005

My green glass butter dish, the subject of this story and a piece of my family's history, is used now as a visual memory trigger when I speak to groups about the value of personal histories. It often strikes an immediate chord with people in the audience and elicits some wonderful stories about everything from secret family recipes to the making of monumental wedding cakes to the medicinal qualities of butter and more. I hope they too will be inspired to preserve the history of a family heirloom or meaningful artefact.

—Annie Payne

A Taste of Life

Annie Payne

My butter dish, made of corrugated green glass, has been a constant fixture on kitchen benches throughout my life, in Brisbane, Adelaide, and now in Perth, Australia. I'm not sure exactly when Mum bought it, or perhaps it was a gift, but everyone's mum seemed to have a similar one sitting on her kitchen bench or table when I was a small child.

During the sultry summer months in Brisbane, Mum had to pop our butter dish into the kerosene fridge on the veranda, or into the icebox, to cool the butter down before serving it at the evening meal. She had a matching green-glass breadbox, in which hand-sliced bread was stored. The breadbox has long vanished from my life. Mum didn't eat bread with her dinner because she, like her French mother, considered it to be "common." Most of the men at our dinner table, however, usually tucked into a slice or two of our freshly baked, wholemeal bread, lavishly spread with Nana's homemade butter fresh from the farm.

When Nana came to stay following my sister's birth, she tied a large apron under my armpits, hoisted me onto a stool at the table's edge, and presented me with a large ceramic bowl. She sifted two cups of flour into the bowl and added a large dollop of golden butter from the green butter dish, then busied herself by beating an egg into a cup of fresh buttermilk.

"Just rub the butter through the flour," she instructed. "Lift your fingers right out of the bowl, letting the buttery flour trickle back into the mixture. Nothing tastes as good as the scone you have made yourself, and these will be wee beauties."

As the ladies gathered for afternoon tea in the sitting room, the men strolled out onto the veranda for a glass or two of icy beer. Nana and I turned the tray of golden scones onto a pretty rose-patterned plate beside the steaming silver teapot, and I proudly nibbled my first scone, piping hot from the oven, with a dab of butter and homemade apricot jam.

Annie Payne

In Adelaide, the problem with the butter in the green glass dish was its hardness, especially on crisp winter days. I was about eight when I began helping Mum prepare for Sunday afternoon tea, a ritual in our home. Grandpa always came, as did some of Mum's friends and Auntie Joan, with as many of her eight children as she could fit into her little Mayflower car.

My task was to make the asparagus rolls—a most complicated job for a small girl wobbling on a stool beside the kitchen bench. Mum had sliced the bread thinly and opened the can of asparagus spears, which were draining in the colander. The next step was to cut off the bread crusts and lightly roll each slice with the rolling pin. I managed these jobs easily, piling the slices into two shaky-looking towers. Then came the buttering of the bread. "Just spread the butter thinly," said Mum, "and make sure you spread it right into the corners."

Easier said than done! I loaded a hard golden chunk of butter onto the knife and lowered it onto the bread, drawing the knife toward me. Disaster! The bread tore as the hard butter clung to the knife. "Just do another one, carefully," snapped Mum, as she filled dainty brandy snaps with cream, keeping a wary eye on the clock.

After five ripped slices were discarded, Mum placed the green glass dish over some hot water to soften the granite-like butter. Ahhh… The power of steam worked its magic and softened the butter into a spreadable consistency. And the remaining bread—sprinkled with grated cheese, topped with an asparagus spear, rolled and fastened with a tooth-pick—turned into a pile of elegant, savoury rolls.

When Mum died, the green glass butter dish came my way, my sister and her family preferring the spreading qualities of margarine to butter. Holding a neat half-pound of butter at the ready, this relic of an earlier era has resided on my kitchen bench since 1979. Its golden butter has been spread on thousands of sandwiches for school lunches, greased countless cake tins, been creamed with sugar to form biscuits and pastries, slathered onto ears of sweet corn, or (best of all) daubed onto a freshly baked scone.

My butter dish is cracked through the bottom now, and the top rim is chipped, but it sits quite harmoniously on the bench top in our 1880s Victorian weatherboard cottage in one of Perth's older, leafier suburbs. My son recently asked if he could have my butter dish, explaining that the "retro" look is big amongst his friends in Sydney. I had to reluctantly decline. I can't quite see this piece of 1940s Australian "kitchenalia" in a slickly modern, minimalist Sydney kitchen.

Soup

Harold Hirshman, Narrator

A smell unlocks a world.

I lift the lid of the chicken soup pot and am assaulted by memories stored somewhere in my nose. The immemori-al mixture of carrots, celery, pepper, bay leaf, and chicken brought to mind my grandmother and the kitchen of my youth. A whiff and they are there, the kitchen and the woman I knew through her works, not her words. Her pies were marvels of precision and efficiency. Chop, chop, chop, roll—cinnamon, lemon juice straight from the bottle, sugar, white Crisco—in no time and without effort, a pie into the oven.

I look at the soup again. I don't remember Grandma skimming it, but she must have. Then she would have turned to the kreplach, little triangles of meat-filled dough. More flour, more rolling until a sheet of millimeter-thin

dough shone on a counter surface. Hands went methodical-
ly to the bowl filled with chopped meat. Drop a ball, drop
another, soldiers in a row. Then the knife quickly cutting
angles. Finally the folding and pressing of the edges, then
on to boiling and frying. All without recipe or appearance
of expending energy. She just did, as I stood and watched.
Why wasn't I out playing ball? Why I watched this silent
woman at her work, I do not know. Now, years later, faced
with dirty dishes absent from my memory kitchen and aided
by omnipresent recipes, I cook.

Harold Hirshman's mother (left) with Grandma Tuts

My mother paid her mother no mind and displayed
none of her craft. In all my years of childhood, she made no
soup, no pie. Perhaps she did kreplach once. Mother was a
woman of words, of speeches, letters, newspapers, cigarettes,

and the telephone. Her culinary efforts were limited to frying or broiling into senselessness a wide variety of meats and thawing an endless array of cardboard-boxed vegetables whose only distinction, one from the other, was in their shape or color. As with many things in my childhood, there were firm rules... No cooked carrots were ever served except for those few added to the peas by the Jolly Green Giant, whose beneficent hand also added a few pieces of pimento to our corn. My mother's one attempt at casserole, served to us children once before our father came home, was greeted with universal 'disacclaim'; its brown groundness in no way suggesting, and thus perfectly honestly proclaiming the absence of, taste. It tasted as brown as it looked. This experiment was put to an end forever when my father arrived home.

"What's for dinner?"

"Casserole."

He surveyed our faces. "What else?"

She didn't even seem disappointed.

Mother reserved her skills for liver, a must in the 1950s if we children were to grow up healthy. Liver's purple brownness represented some kind of rebuke to my mother's aesthetics, a rebuke that could only be requited when the meat had been cooked to a real brownness and achieved the texture of Buster Brown's shoes. It's no wonder that I abjured eating my grandmother's chopped liver based on experiencing my mother's liver expertise. I should have known better. I watched Grandma prepare it. The liver had barely been in the pan when its still reddish flesh was ground with onions and eggs in a cast-iron machine reserved for this ritual, then mixed with chicken fat. How could it be bad?

So as I approach this pot of chicken soup, I bring my history—a mixture of words and memory. I usually cook from a book and try to arrange all the ingredients in a row, having carefully shopped with a list so that I can be sure everything will be in its place. Even the French bread I have made many times, I do not have in my memory. I check the recipe and the proportions and newly reacquaint myself with the rising times and the baking regimen of a very hot oven, whose dry interior is moistened with ice cubes propitiously tossed on its floor. But for chicken soup, each time I forget and search in vain for a recipe. I never queried my taciturn grandmother as to her magic. I had two eyes and a partly opened heart, which sufficed to keep with me the cherished ingredients, more or less. The main outlines are there. Carrots and celery were joined with turnips during my first marriage. But didn't Grandma use a clove of garlic? How many peppercorns? As to salt, even if I'd asked, she couldn't have told me. Plenty, more than doctors now allow.

However badly remembered, the smell is close enough to bring up the story of these two women. A mother and daughter who were so far apart, so different, yet whose lives were so overlapped that they talked every day, saw each other almost every day, and always lived within a few blocks of each other. My mother was tall and slender, my grand-mother short and robust. Grandma never ate but always maintained her weight. There was an aura of tragedy in my grandmother's life. A son had died soon after birth. My mother was to die in early middle age, and although

Grandma could not have known this, she lived as though she expected it.

I never understood their relationship, how a mother could fail to learn essential crafts from her mother. What well of distance set my mother down a path so far away from her mother's skills? What ambition in my grandmother propelled my mother to abandon the kitchen (a kitchen notorious for its silent effort) for the words.

Grandma and I had a fierce battle after my mother's death. We were sitting in a tearoom, when such things still existed, talking of eating habits. In particular whether we, as a family, had kept kosher outside of the house, as we were doing at the time of the conversation. "Of course," my grandmother said.

"But don't I remember you and Mother eating hamburgers at White Mansion?" (A greasy spoon near my father's plant.)

"Absolutely not," she answered, a flash of anger cracking her reserve. "Your mother always kept kosher!"

Too young to desist, I piled memory on memory, only to be met by a deepening fury. My apostasy was never to be forgiven. The comradeship of pies did not permit deviation from hagiography. Piety was sacred, and memory would just have to be shaped with the same firmness shown the kreplach.

I taste the soup; the past is recaptured. Next Yom Kippur, French bread with a little butter will join the soup to form a non-kosher beginning to an ancient fast. As I await the meal, I pick up my pen to turn memory smells into words, honoring both women.

Maria Barr is a woman in her thirties who was diagnosed with advanced breast cancer four years ago. Our numerous conversations, which took place over a year's time, produced a narrative describing her treatment for cancer. As well as her medical experiences, Maria talked about her family, her job, and the complexities of juggling the demands placed on her. The following is an excerpt that speaks to the nature of caregiving and the generosity of one doctor in particular. Maria kept a journal. We adapted her journal entries and our conversations to that format to best relay her story. With the exception of Maria, all names are fictitious.

—Christine Harland Chamberlain

Finding Maria

Maria Barr, Narrator

Waiting is something I've done a lot of since my diagnosis. I don't want to read the magazines or look around at other people in the waiting room. Instead, I bring along my little book full of empty white pages that I hope I'll have the days to fill. I always choose a chair by the window, a way of being here and not being here.

Not long ago in time, but ages ago in life, I sat in a room just past the door over there, waiting to hear the results of my surgery. My right breast was still black and blue and very sore. I was in a gown, sitting on the table; my husband was on the chair. The moment was so big that we sat without talking. There was a rustle outside, the sound of my chart coming out of the tray, and the surgeon, Dr. Mark, anxious and a little distracted, came through the door. His face gave him away. I found myself feeling sorry for him.

They had not been able to get clean margins, he told us. The nodes they removed were dirty. The cancer was aggressive, and they would do a radical mastectomy followed by chemotherapy and radiation. We sat in silence. I began to cry. In the past, Dr. Mark had always ended our appointments saying, "We'll take good care of you here." He didn't say it this time, and I was suddenly sure that I was going to die.

It may seem odd to describe myself in my journal, but the fact is I can hardly remember what Maria was like before cancer. I remember someone very in charge, someone who gave 120 percent all the time. There was a Maria who was sometimes impatient, always efficient, always in control.

This Maria needed help.

Maria Barr (left) and Christine Chamberlain

Wednesday

I'm back in my sunny corner, waiting to see my oncologist. I had a three o'clock appointment, and it is now after four. I can say for certain that the old, hard-driving Maria wouldn't have waited an hour or two or three for anyone, but all of us here know that one of Dr. Lary's greatest gifts as a doctor is his willingness to give time. If he is late now, it is because he is spending time with someone who needs him. We all know how that feels.

Dr. Lary has taught me a lot about quality time. Just this morning I stopped to think about it. It was to be a very full day. I was coming to the hospital, so I wanted to get to work early. I called to my son Bobby upstairs, but he didn't come down. And he didn't come down. I grew nervous as the minutes ticked by. I stormed up and found him sitting in a chair, his shoes untied, his hair uncombed, playing with one of his games. I was irritated and impatient. He cried.

Now, sitting here at the end of the day, I know that what my son needed was a little quiet time. I could have sent him off to school peacefully; instead, I sent him off feeling incomplete.

I have never known Dr. Lary's gaze to drift away from mine while I'm talking. I've never seen him rearrange the papers on his desk or let a hint of irritation cross his face. He doesn't get out of his chair to let me know that our appointment is over. For our time together, he is always present in the moment. He is really with me. The key, I think, is that he focuses. The people in the waiting room, the telephone calls that need to be answered, the patient he has just seen or the one who is coming in, seem to disappear, and together we concentrate on making me better. He is a peaceful presence in which I can ask all my questions, allay my fears, and feel like a human being.

At the end of that time, he leans across the desk, looks me in the eye and says, "Do you have any other questions, Maria?" I leave his office feeling complete.

I know that Dr. Lary has a big schedule every day and that most days are very difficult for him because his patients are in a hard place. It feels as though he manages time with his heart, he does what feels right. Because he focuses on what is before him, he really finishes one appointment before moving on to the next. We all feel better. It is worth the wait.

Friday

I wish that I didn't have to come here at all, but since I do, I have to say that it is very pleasant. One of the comforting aspects of the environment is that it is small and personal. Everyone speaks to me. People smile and seem happy to see me. It is also physically pretty, full of sun and color. When I come in, the women who work here talk to me about all sorts of things—kids, clothes, weather, work. It is never "Poor Maria." It is "Hi, you look nice today." I need that. I need to be a person outside of cancer.

The receptionists and nurses are very humane. They notice and remember patients as individuals. I believe that's because they really care. Sometimes when I tell my husband something and he doesn't remember, I am impatient because I believe that means he isn't interested enough to bother. This is the other side of the coin. People here remember us because they are invested.

Not long ago, I told everyone at the bank where I work that for a week we were all going to find something nice to say to every customer who came in. When a woman walked by my desk the other day, I told her how pretty she looked in the color she was wearing. She turned and gave me a nice smile. An elderly gentleman made an innocent remark about my very short hair, and I told him that I had just finished chemotherapy. He seemed embarrassed and left quickly.

The next day he came back and sat down at my desk.

"I appreciated your telling me about yourself," he said. "I wanted to tell you that I have prostate cancer, and I do understand. If you have the courage to be open, I should, too."

Those little things we say to each other, sometimes to perfect strangers, make us all feel less lonely. We all want to believe that people care. Kind words make a big difference to fear or pain or loneliness. I learned that here. The old Maria was always polite, but I'm not sure that she was always compassionate.

Tuesday

Even though the Herceptin seems to be working, and I have days when I feel back to my old self, the fact that I have cancer is with me all the time. It's a presence that walks by my side, and I think that will be true all my life. Some of it is fear. Some of it is that now, at thirty-six, if I make it to fifty I have been given a gift. Some of it is hating to be without a breast. Once in a while, that gets on top of me. The last time I went in to see Dr. Lary, I was feeling very low.

They weighed me and gave me my gown. Then I sat in the little consulting room, having been there more times than I like to think.

Dr. Lary came in and was looking at my chart when he asked, "How are you, Maria?"

"I'm all right."

In an instant, Dr. Lary stopped what he was doing and came over to me. Holding my arm, he looked carefully at me and said, "Maria, tell me what's wrong." He not only listens, he hears—not only what I say, but what I don't say. He could choose to pass over the little things he notices, but that never happens. He never seems to think, I have ten minutes, and I don't have time to stop for this now.

There have been times when I wondered whether I imagined his compassion. Was I, after all, just another patient, just a chart full of numbers and results? And was he particularly adept at being charming? Then one day Dr. Lary stepped out of the room for a moment. Feeling like a naughty child, I reached over and lifted the last page of my chart. At the bottom of the page, after his report, he had written, "It continues to be my good fortune to be part of this young woman's care." He hadn't written it for me, he hadn't written it for anyone in particular. He had put that down because that's how he felt. It meant the world to me.

Sometimes I thank him for getting me through, for saving my life.

"No, Maria," he always tells me. "It's you. You've done the work."

Living Life, Learning Lessons

Mary Ann Merksamer, Narrator

I have lived a privileged life, blessed with love and beauty around me. I have been a lifelong student and teacher, so I have shared deeply with many wonderful people.

When I was lucky enough to break my leg at the age of eighteen, I found out that there were more questions than answers in this world. Until then, I never questioned much. Everything before had gone according to schedule, and my programming had been fairly standard. Eighteen months in a cast and having to drop out of the University of Colorado and attend Sacramento State College made me start thinking about life and its meaning. Since that time, I believe I have remained open to new ideas, new experiences, and new paths.

Mary Ann practicing Tai Chi

In the 1960s, in search of the physical balance I had lost because of my broken leg, I discovered yoga and T'ai Chi Ch'uan. I managed to find balance for a time, but learned ever so much more about my body, control, letting go, and just being. At the same time, I ran into some far-out thinking people who were exploring "humanistic psychology." What they said resonated in me: It was the person, not the label, the experience, not the rule, and the feeling, not the logic, that had authentic meaning.

As a therapist throughout my twenties, I experimented with these ideas, listened to others, talked, and provided experiences for many people who began their own introspection. One of my teachers during this time was Ram Dass, whose speeches I listened to and whose books I read. Another was Leland Johnson, the father of my lifelong joy—my son Marc.

Leland and I traveled throughout the United States, Mexico, and Europe, teaching some of what we knew and learning about what we didn't know. It was a magical time of expansion of consciousness. Silly as it may sound, I can't use that phrase without clarifying that we were not using drugs to do the expansion. We used group gatherings and innovative, experiential learning such as role-playing, dancing, musical expression, chanting, singing, bells, prayer bowls, and more to guide our emotional states. In those turbulent times, we were seeking a more peaceful and accepting world, hoping idealistically that our efforts would lead to real change in our society.

Looking back now in 2003, I realize that nearly all the "new, experiential, humanistic experiences" we were designing and working with have been almost fully integrated into the existing social structures. Fitness centers teach yoga and T'ai Chi. Meditation is respected as an experience that can make a positive difference in one's health and attitude, stress level, and even problem-solving. Dance and singing groups abound to support people loosening the logical structure of their lives, to encourage and support balance with nurturing creative juices. Nutrition and exercise are valued and encouraged for both physical and mental fitness. The body and mind are no longer considered separate entities.

The one thing that probably has not changed enough is the belief that going to a therapist is an indication of mental defect or of a person not being strong enough. It is natural for people to evolve during their lifetime. To do so, we need new experiences, mentors, teachers, and the like. It is not failure to seek a coach.

I am very proud to have been on the forefront of the winds of change. I met the people who wrote the books, played with them, and learned from them. One of my most glowing experiences was bringing Alan Watts to Houston to give a lecture followed the next day by a small seminar for professionals at our growth center, Espiritu. I picked up the philosopher and his wife at the airport. When a security guard in Baggage Claim asked for their tickets, Alan said he didn't have them but could identify everything in his bag. Unlatching his suitcase, he said the first item would be the top of an oxygen tank with a brass stick. He pulled out the tank top and began hitting it with the stick, making a really loud **G-O-N-G** that reverberated throughout Baggage Claim.

People began to gather and watch Alan pull unusual items from his bag and use them in unusual ways. He had gongs, chanting machines (harmoniums), bells, kimonos, and obis to wear at his lectures and seminars. The security guard nudged me and asked me to get my father out of there. "He's not my father," I said, "and I didn't ask him to identify his possessions. You had better find a way to do it yourself, or we're likely to be here for quite awhile."

Every spring during the 1970s, we gathered people together for a celebration of spring solstice. Sufi drummers, dancers, chanters, large circles of people would move freely in the meadows with joy in their hearts. At the time, it was the only collaborative effort to bring multiple organizations together, including our Espiritu group, Billie Gollnick's yoga students, and the 3HO group with Sadhu Singh Khalsa, the founder of their Total Health Recovery Program. Satya Singh Khalsa handled the planning and publicity.

My greatest learning came in the kitchen during one of those celebrations. I was cubing watermelon for the fruit salad when Satya said that we needed to take all the seeds out as a way of honoring our guests. I thought she was nuts; that was going to be an enormous amount of work. Hours later, I understood that our engaging in the meditative seed removal was a transformative experience. Doing for others to enhance their experience, with no expectation of gratitude or acknowledgments, is an experience of selflessness.

To this day, I continue to do similar little things for friends and guests in my home as a way of honoring their presence in my life. We could give it a name—karma yoga. But the label doesn't come close to the meaning.

The Sufi drummers took us away into the drumbeats, moving us through the essential rhythms of life energy each spring. It was impossible to block out those primitive feelings, movements, and pulsations. They took each of us through multiple emotional transformations. Our only rule was no drugs. Sometimes I just have to repeat this because so many people associate these images with drugged-out hippies. That is *not* what we were. We simply were exploring the full extent of our humanness.

Leland and I shared this learning and teaching process throughout the 1960s and into the 1970s. Throughout my thirty-five years as a therapist, one lesson from that era influenced all my work: One cannot be forced to learn, or to feel better about oneself, or to understand. One can facilitate, generate an environment of safety, be present and attentive, and be *evocative*. One cannot and should not ever be *provocative*. It is a subtle difference, but one of the most basic in the world of therapy, counseling, and teaching.

Mary Ann Merksamer,
grace and beauty,
two weeks before she died

As a personal historian, I've always called ethical wills "Life Letters" because they are not legal documents, they cover more than ethics, and, although they can become codicils to a will, they are more about life than death: gifts from the living to the living about living. Life Letters can be prepared as separate documents or as part of a larger personal history. In either case, the intent is to dip beneath the "this and that happened" stories to make sense out of what happened, to assess the meaning and value of experience, and to convey wisdom, wishes, and blessings. As a sixtieth birthday gift, I audio-recorded the life story of Kathryn Neustadter, my friend of over thirty-five years and a pillar of her rural community. The closing chapter of her book—but certainly not her life—is her Life Letter, an excerpt from which follows. In "Reflections on Life So Far," she shares some of what she has learned with her two daughters.

—Linda Blachman

Kathryn Neustadter's Life Letter

I have wondered over the course of my life how religions that propose to make people better can do such horrible things in their name. Why can't we all love one another? My feeling about religions is that they're spokes of a wheel, so they all go to the same place. It's just how you get there. I don't understand why people care which spoke anyone is on when they're all needed to create the wheel.

How can man be so cruel and inhuman to man? I think things are really bad in the world, and yet I haven't rushed out to improve life for millions of people. I became politically active in the Vietnam War (a lot of peace marching) and kept that up for the first year of my marriage. Then I stopped. I feel like we should all be political in a way. I also believe in trying to do unto others as they would do unto you. Of course, I come up against it as a mere mortal. One of my guilt complexes is that I really should make the world better for people and do lots of good things, one of which is to help the less fortunate. These things weigh on me. I feel guilty about not being active enough politically, but for my health and well-being and my family, I just can't do it. I don't think you can be perfect.

I would like my children to understand that to give to others and to do things for people is very rewarding. It's a form of personal growth, but it shouldn't be a guilt trip. As I've gotten older, I'm feeling less guilty about what I've not done.

I also think that the world is a big place, we're only a little speck in the whole scheme of things, so whatever we do with a good heart is probably good. As Mother Teresa said, "We cannot do great things in this life. We can only do small things with great love."

I can't understand the great love and the great giving that the people in my life have poured out to me. They say it's because of what I've given them. But I don't know what that is. I've given them fun; I've given them friendship. Oh, I feed them, and I've given them a lot of gag gifts for stocking stuffers. I've been here for them, but I never feel like I've been here for them as much as they've been here for me. And I'm not being pious. The power of what they've shown and given me is unbelievable.

I have done a lot in the community, and I think that I've done some good for people. I started a preschool that was meaningful to a lot of families. I did what I loved, and I did it as well as I could. Sometimes I thought I could have been a better teacher. Other times, I thought I was the best. The chamber music series is something I started and that I love. Other people seem to like it, so they feel that I've done a great thing for them. It's nice to know that I've done all these things without saying, "I'm going to make our town better." Something was here and ripe to happen. I worked with a great group of people, and we did it and had fun for the most part.

If given another twenty years, I would like to continue what I'm doing because I love it. I'd also like to become more proficient at the things I like to do. I might volunteer at the preschool. I want to do more photography and more entertaining and cooking. I've told everybody, "Just have your parties over here. I've got the house!"

Then I would like to see if there's something else out there that I could do. I'm not too old to be in the Peace Corps, but I fear losing my creature comforts. So there are things that tickle my fancy, yet the challenge is too great for me to make the effort. I want my own bathroom.

Right now, I'm in a settled mode. I think you kids like me better because I'm not freneti-cally running around doing

Kathryn "Kit" Bercovici Neustadter

things. I'll sit and talk; I'll relax. I'm more available. I'm certain-ly working on that. I'm also more available to myself.

The most important lesson I've learned from life is to be present with it. It took a lot of learning. I've learned to sit down and enjoy little things and not say I've got to get up and do some task first. I used to get frustrated… "Clean that up first and then have fun!" "Help me now and then have fun!" I think you need to live your life.

I do like not feeling stressed right now. That's great, guys! Remember that. Do what you can and enjoy a full and powerful life, but don't overdo. There's a balance, I guess. It takes a long time to find it. So kids, that's my goal and my wish: Find your balance. Be empathetic and caring and good to yourselves. I know both of you guys do that more than I do, so you're well on the road. You two are great. You're wise enough.

Now, I can say I'm very, very happy to be satisfied with what I've done. I feel like I need to push myself in some respects because you don't close down and say, "Okay, I did that; it's all over." But I did do a lot. That's how I grew up. My grandfather was an incredibly civic-minded person. My aunt was. My uncle was. My mother was not. Basically, she had me, she lived her life, she enjoyed some stuff, and she did her art. She didn't move out into the community. But that was her life.

So we each do what we do, and I don't think we are that important. In the scheme of life, we're only here for a short time. That's sort of hard to grasp. If you settle on it too much, you can just sort of do nothing. On the other hand, you can't fight it.

I do feel that I have been the same person throughout my life, but I think I've grown. I feel a little wiser since your dad died, mellower and more accepting, seeing things with more perspective and valuing what I've done. I feel stronger, more comfortable with myself.

So I think we should strive to do the best we can and accept it. What's that thing we all learned in school? *The Serenity Prayer:* I strive to accept what I cannot change, to change what I can, and to know the difference. The prayer didn't mean anything to me then, but it means something now. If I can change something, wow.

I've been very grateful for my security, the people I've known, and the life I've been allowed to lead—a life with a lot of satisfaction and a lot of room for growth and creativity. Emotionally, I struggled as a kid, had a "bad" childhood and did a lot of whining in the interim, but life's been pretty easy for me with lots of satisfaction. I didn't have to fight that hard for what I got. I feel really blessed and would hope that happens for you kids.

I'd like to be remembered as "The Gag Gift Lady!" But for deeper meaning, I think I'd like to be remembered for just having been a good mother. I don't know if I was or wasn't. I sort of ran the job by the seat of my pants and didn't agonize over what's a good mother, what's a bad mother. Agonizing was not my thing, so I think I made a lot of mistakes. But I hope the mothering that you guys had was better than average.

For me, motherhood was sometimes hard work. People said, "Motherhood is a part of life, but you have to make something more of your life intellectually." I thought that a lot because I'm more than a cow, but the cow part I loved! So motherhood was very meaningful in an organic way. It was enough. Let's put it this way… Being a mother and raising both of you were probably the prime events in my life.

I love you both really deeply.

Take care, Mom

I wrote this story in 2004 while leading my first reminiscence writing group, following the model laid out by James Birren and Kathryn Cochran in Telling the Stories of Life Through Guided Autobiography Groups. *My students ranged from a twenty-one-year-old sex worker to a ninety-one-year-old fundamentalist preacher. That first class taught me that holding space for the sharing of life's stories is one of the simplest and most powerful things a personal historian can do. I will always include reminiscence writing groups in my repertoire, so I can continue to learn from the experiences of others and continue to practice my own autobiographical writing.*

—Sarah White

The Plunge

Sarah White

We were in Marty's Volkswagen van, headed for
Griffey Reservoir outside Bloomington, Indiana, on
a hot summer day in 1974. The usual gang had assembled
for the trip—Marty driving, me in the passenger seat keeping him company over the engine's roar, Donna, Colette,
Rick, and his brother Victor in the back. In our long hair
and tie-dyes, we might have stepped from an R. Crumb cartoon.

I had known these people a little over a year. In that
time, in this same rickety van, I had made who knows how
many pilgrimages to Bloomington. We would look up our
older friends already in college there, confident of finding a
place to hang out. Someone who could purchase a jug of red
wine for us. We had used Bloomington as home base for
adventures for the better part of a year. Trips to hike the
woods, to go down in the caves, and today, to go skinny-dipping at the reservoir.

I was chattering with Marty as always, but inside, agony
began to brew.

Skinny-dipping. Fat me, thin them.

Where would I find the nerve to take off my clothes in
front of my friends, all just slightly hipper than me? Could I
get *fat-ly* naked in front of the people I admired most in the world?

I have been fat for as long as I have been looking up to
other people.

It began in Carmel with Janet across the street. I followed her lead from my first steps on. I must have been

about nine, and she thirteen, when she began insisting I eat supper with her. Her mother and father worked long hours down in the city. They got home late and prepared adult meals that they sat down to after cocktails at our bedtime.

So as 5:00 p.m. approached each day, just before she went home, the housekeeper would heat up something for Janet from the store—usually chicken with noodles from a wide-mouthed jar. Janet hated to eat alone and pleaded with me to join her. I would hurry to finish so I could get home in time for supper at my own house.

Not surprisingly, I began to gain weight. My mother suspected candy jags and cut my allowance. I kept gaining weight, and I kept my secret about why. Ten pounds turned to twenty and more. I don't know why I was powerless to tell Janet I wanted to stop eating with her, but I was.

By the time I was twelve, I carried over 150 pounds on my 5-foot body. Those next years were punctuated with the embarrassing moments of fat people... Shopping in women's departments, where the clothes didn't look like what other young girls wore. Attempts to purchase bathing suits. The pants that split at the thigh or seat at random, public intervals.

Then, at age fifteen, catharsis. I broke my leg, and somehow that gave me permission to break other things. I broke off my relationship with Janet. No more bowls of noodles before supper.

Not long after that, I began the Great Hot Dog Diet. My buddy Sue had read about it in a teen magazine. Our mothers agreed to let us try. We opted out of family meals for all of a summer and most of the school year beyond. We drank Carnation instant breakfast drink and ate only hot dogs, hot dogs, hot dogs—no buns, no condiments. The pounds wore away, in twos and threes and fives. I began to buy my clothes where the other girls did. But inside I knew I was still fat.

Sometime in the next year, I met Marty at the YMCA, and he introduced me to his friends Colette and Donna. Then we met Victor and Rick at a Bible study group. When they secretly confessed they'd rather be smoking a joint than reading the Bible, our six-way friendship was formed. Just as I'd broken off with Janet, I left Sue and the hot dog diet behind, and began roaming with my new friends.

I graduated a semester early from high school and went to work for an insurance company as a typist. I continued to diet and exercise, avoiding the morning donuts in the cafeteria and pacing the fence during my half-hour lunch breaks.

"I'm down to 119 pounds!" I announced excitedly during one break-time, when the ladies all gathered in the restroom to suck down cigarettes and talk.

"Then why do you still look fat?" responded one of those smoker typists in her gravelly voice; one of those blunt Hoosier farmwomen who would not think to dissemble or flatter a young-un like me.

"I don't know!" I wailed. But I knew what she said was true. I had no breasts to speak of yet—I could still pass the Ann Landers pencil test, but my hips were as wide as the county. I had stretch marks instead of the multiple tummies of the year before. Still, my figure was totally unlike the Twiggy-thin girls on TV.

And now here I was, with my furry-freak friends on my way through Bloomington to a date with nudity, in my 119-pound fat body.

We arrived at the parking area for the reservoir and began hiking back to the swimming hole. If you've seen the movie *Breaking Away*, you can picture the scenery—a trail through a mix of hardwoods and pines, leading to the spot where sun-bleached limestone cliffs ring sparkling blue water.

Not one of us carried a towel roll.

We reached a promontory where quarried limestone made steps connecting the overlook to the water's edge. We sat down to smoke a joint. Then some of my friends began dropping clothes and diving over the edge.

Could I? Would I?

Time stopped for me in the middle of that steamy, Indiana summer day. A voice spoke inside my head, borrowing the gravelly voice of that smoker typist.

If you don't do this, your whole life will be just like this. You'll be on the sidelines, pretending you don't mind that other people are having fun and you're not. Is that what you want?

"No."

These are your best friends. What could you possibly lose by taking off your clothes right now? What is that worth compared to what you might gain?

"Nothing."

I stood up and took off my clothes.

I wasn't the last one in. Someone probably witnessed my butt wobble as I ran and dived, but now I don't remember who. What I remember, as vividly as that voice in my head, is the sensation that followed:

I am in the middle of the lake doing a dead-man's float. Naked Marty and the others are drifting nearby. In my peripheral vision, I see a rim of stone topped with green forest. It makes a perfect circle around me, topped by the dome of the cloudless blue sky.

I am seventeen, and I am in a beautiful place surrounded by people I love and who love me in the best sense of that word. Together, we can do anything—even bare ourselves.

Sarah White, at age seventeen,
giving the "stink-eye" to the photographer

Courtney Chambers seemingly had everything going against her. She was an African American from a single-parent family in a school with few minorities, a student with cognitive disabilities and a stuttering problem attending special education classes. Yet she was in everything and did everything. For the La Crosse School District's monthly television program, KidsFirst, I interviewed Courtney five times from eighth grade through her senior year. Always, she had something to say. I so admired this young woman that, as her graduation gift, I created a customized book over the Internet that included her story and numerous photos I had taken over the years. Then she amazed everyone with an exceptionally moving speech on graduation day, which later was shared with the community. In the end, I reprinted the book to include her speech and the reaction of others.

—Susan T. Hessel

Somewhere Along the Way
The Inspiring Life of Courtney Chambers

Susan T. Hessel

Somewhere along the way, eighteen-year-old Courtney Chambers stopped listening to those who told her what she *couldn't* do. And there were plenty of them. Instead, she listened to the voice inside her that said she *could* do much more than anyone imagined.

Someone with cognitive disabilities in band and the show choir? Volunteering with organizations that promote academic excellence? Courtney did all those activities and more—acting in a school play, working backstage for another, and performing in the Logan High School's Madrigal Dinner to raise money for the choir department. She also worked part-time and went on a church mission trip to the Dominican Republic, where she taught crocheting so effectively that teachers back home asked her to show them how.

As I learned during my interview sessions over the years for the school district's television program, *KidsFirst*, Courtney accomplished still more as a student in La Crosse, Wisconsin. Although she had a stutter, her hand was the first up to be interviewed, and she had plenty to say. She spoke before the city council about the dangers of teen smoking and, at the Wisconsin State Capitol, advocated for those with disabilities—two subjects she knew well. She served on her school's Senior Leadership Team and volunteered to work with parents to create a new Logan Legacy Scholarship. It was no surprise when she offered to present the scholarship to students at convocation with me, the parent of another graduate.

I had no idea, though, that this wonderful young woman had done the unthinkable. She applied to be a student speaker at graduation, the first special education student to do so. As she said later, "All my life, I saw people doing things and winning things, and I was never homecoming queen or prom queen. I just wanted to prove that I could do this." A committee anonymously reviewed the proposed speeches, selecting three from the usual suspects—highly successful students labeled from birth: "Most likely to give graduation speeches."

The three students gave fine speeches, probably much like the ones their peers delivered at commencements across the country. Moms and dads were proud. Excited soon-to-be graduates listened before they received their diplomas, posed for photos, and celebrated. When it came time for his address, Principal Scott Mihalovic called Courtney to the podium. He told the seniors of Courtney's desire to speak to her class and how she had responded to her disappointment about not being selected by working harder on her speech. "Fair was not equal," Mihalovic said. Then he announced that his time to speak was going to Courtney so she could deliver her appropriately titled speech, "Never Give Up." Students, parents, grandparents, and staff visibly took notice as Courtney rose to speak.

When Mr. Mihalovic told me that my speech had not been selected, I felt kind of upset and disappointed. I decided instead of feeling bad, I was NOT going to give up. I did some more work on my speech and went back to Mr. Mihalovic. Never giving up has made me who I am today.

I have a cognitive disability and take special education classes. Sometimes I stutter when I get excited or nervous. I've really worked hard these past four years in high school. This year I especially worked hard on my grades, and it shows because I have a 3.9 GPA.

There are people who don't have confidence in me, but I have proven them wrong by standing up tonight and delivering this speech.

Having a disability is hard because people look at you and see you in those classes and call you names. One day, somebody asked me what it's like to have a disability. It's hard because you learn at a different pace. I really hate it when people call people with a disability names. It just means that we need extra help. Everyone needs help with something because in this world we are not all perfect. Everyone here needs help with something. The difference between you and me is that I don't know what you need help with.

After Courtney wished her classmates well, advising them to never give up, the senior class rose as one to give her a standing ovation. Parents cheered for her with tears in their eyes. At that moment in La Crosse, "respect" was spelled C-O-U-R-T-N-E-Y C-H-A-M-B-E-R-S.

Richard Mial, Opinion Page Editor for the *La Crosse Tribune*, wrote a column about Courtney's speech: "An interesting thing happened at my son's graduation Saturday from Logan High School. Students and audience members got an unexpected lesson from an unexpected place…

Focus on what people can do, not what they can't do. And don't give up. Those are good messages, no matter who is giving the speech." Judging from readers' responses to Mial's article, Courtney's message touched even more people within our community.

Courtney Chambers as a college student

Courtney is now enrolled at Western Technical College in La Crosse, where she is studying early childhood development in the hopes of one day owning a childcare center. If she earns an associate degree there, she will be the first student with cognitive disabilities to do so. And no one counts her out. When the going gets hard, and her classes are challenging, Courtney fights on with a magnificent smile.

The La Crosse Community Foundation honored Courtney with a 2006 Building a Foundation for Our Community Award, which is given to three young people a year for "leadership in transforming opportunities into community service and action." The award honors community service, giving each recipient five hundred dollars toward his or her continuing education costs plus another five hundred dollars to be donated to charities of the recipient's choice. Courtney's charitable award money went to her church for another mission trip, to the African Drum Program at Logan High School, and to the local Hunger Taskforce. Because of her incredible wealth of spirit, and because she refused to listen to the naysayers, Courtney has joined the ranks of older, better known philanthropists. Bill Gates, founder of Microsoft and one of the world's great philanthropists, once said, "Is the rich world aware of how four billion of the six billion live? If we were aware, we would want to help out; we'd want to get involved."

As philanthropist Courtney Chambers said, equally eloquently, "I like to help out in our nice community. I like it a lot."

This story is an excerpt from Being the Rock (Populore), a tribute to the author's son Bob Harding and a chronicle of their lives together since a traumatic brain injury left Bob a spastic quadriplegic over twenty years ago when he was a high school senior. Their joint memoir is about the immensity of love, devotion, and responsibility, and what it means to hold one another up—to be a "rock"—through times of struggle. The "Bob Hardings" of the world are often overlooked when it comes to gathering personal histories; they must rely on the love and care of their guardians and family to ensure both the quality of their lives and the preservation of their life stories. How fortunate Bob is to have a father interested in preserving his son's legacy of perseverance, despite his father's own physical challenges. (Macular degeneration has left Richard legally blind.)

A team provided writing and production services for this project, including over ten hours of interviews with Richard, Bob, and Bob's caregivers. The writing process—helping Richard find and capture the right words, despite his obstacles in writing them down—deepened and enriched the resonance of the final product. And what a lesson their story is for the rest of us.

—Rae Jean Sielen

Our Secret Code

Richard D. Harding, Narrator

When describing what it was like in the early stages of his rehabilitation, Bob now says, "I felt like the real Helen Keller." Spasticity caused involuntary tightness and stiffness in his vocal cords that rendered him unable to speak. And while he was in Nashville, he developed a condition in which bacteria filaments grew from his pupils to the inside of his eyelids, obstructing his vision and causing the horrible sensation of having sand in his eyes.

Without his voice, sight, or muscle control, there was just no way for Bob to communicate. The frustration level between us was high. We did what we could. I'd sit with him and tell him that I loved him. I'd ask him if he needed food or water and if he was comfortable, but it was always a guessing game. I remember so clearly the frustration radiating from his eyes. It was obvious how badly he wanted to be able to say something, but he was basically trapped inside his own body.

When we were finally able to develop a communication system, it improved everything by a thousandfold—our relationship, our happiness, and Bob's health. I noticed another young person in the hospital in Nashville who was using an alphabet board to communicate. I thought there must be some way we could develop a system like that. Instead of vocalizing words, the boy would spell them by pointing to the letters he saw on the board. Bob was unable to see or point, but he could overcome his spasticity enough to squeeze my hand, and that was all we needed.

Bob, a gifted athlete,
before his football accident

I put my hand in his and said, "Bob, we're going to find a way to communicate. We will do whatever is easiest for you." I described the board to him, and we settled on breaking down the alphabet into six sections. To speak with Bob now, you hold his hand and say, "A to F, G to L, M to R, S to X, Y, and Z." Bob squeezes your hand as you speak the section he needs. Then you say the letters in that particular section; for example, "G, H, I, J, K, L." He squeezes again on the letter he needs. Then you begin the whole process over again for the next letter.

We tinkered with this process for about two months before we had it all ironed out. Sometimes, if the spasticity is too much and his hand gets tired, he'll spell by moving the big toe on his right foot instead of squeezing your hand. (A while back he decided to name that toe Mr. Motormouth.) In a way, it's kind of like we have a secret code.

It sounds tedious, but the system has been very successful. We got *fast*. Bob occasionally uses a computerized speaking device called a Pathfinder instead of communicating one on one by hand, but the computer is just not as fast. Especially now, since we're able to manage his muscle tone so well with the various medications, Bob can really fly through the scanning and spelling. He composes long, complicated sentences, phrase after phrase, and if he thinks you're guessing what he's about to say, he'll switch the wording around or throw in an extra adjective just to keep you on your toes. He doesn't let anyone put words in his mouth.

We can be in a noisy, crowded restaurant, talking and scanning at the table. As soon as Bob finishes what he's saying, he'll comment on things that he overheard or observed at other tables around us while he was spelling. All at once, he's managing the spasticity and the pain with his breathing, listening to what you're saying in conversation, remembering what he wants to say in long sentences, and controlling the squeezing as you scan the alphabet. To top it all off, he's also aware of everything that's going on in the room around him.

The first time Bob went to his dentist in Morgantown after we got this system working, we discovered how versatile a communication tool it was. The dentist was wearing a mask and gloves to work on Bob. He had one hand on Bob's jaw as he used the other to inject Novocain. I couldn't be close enough to Bob to "talk" in our usual way, but I could see Mr. Motormouth. Watching his toe, I was able to translate Bob's non-vocal comment to the doctor, "Dr. J., this is a new-tasting Novocain."

The doctor's eyes above the mask opened very wide. Then he said, "That's remarkable! Never have I had both hands in a patient's mouth, along with a syringe, and the patient's been able to communicate. That's one for my diary!"

I didn't really know what to expect when Bob came out of the coma. The fact that he couldn't speak was devastating. He wasn't the same person to me; I couldn't know what was going on inside him. Now, he can pinpoint and describe his pain and needs, which has helped immeasurably in fine-tuning his medications (as well as his happiness and quality of life). Finding a way to bypass his most obvious physical

Richard and Bob on a road trip in the White Mountains of Vermont

limitations and tap into his personality and intelligence opened up a whole new world to us... We could finally see Bob's bright potential and look at him as a person instead of as a collection of handicaps.

When Bob asks questions, I no longer ask myself before answering, *Will he understand?* I talk to him as if there had been no accident on the football field that day. I know and sense that he has emotions and feelings and concerns for his family that have never changed, and I know he has a deep-seated interest in me. He also takes an active interest in the people around him and truly enjoys helping others when he can. For example, his nursing home needed a new popcorn machine, and he bought it for them. He also provided the bird sanctuary and a 1,200-light Christmas tree for the lobby.

Bob is remarkable in that he makes maximum use of what God has given him.

Richard and Bob, circa 2006

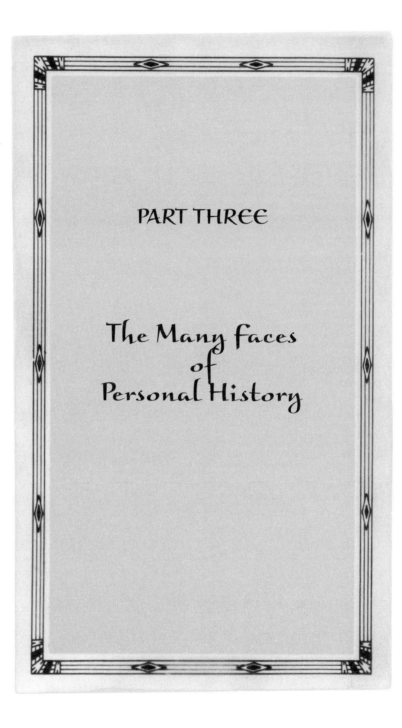

PART THREE

The Many Faces of Personal History

Introduction

W ithin the format of the printed page, you will discover many faces to personal history.

First, we must choose a voice for the story—first person (I was born), second person (you were born), or third person (he or she was born). Catherine Munson speaks for herself in "Sand Hills Murder Mystery," a first-person narrative drawn from an oral history interview conducted by Trena Cleland. Oral history transcripts are likely to stick pretty close to the interview as it was recorded, editing out only repetitious and throat-clearing phrases such as "Well, then…" and "you know." The personal historian is more likely to edit an oral history interview for narrative flow.

The point in a first-person story is to capture the narrator's voice and viewpoint. Sometimes a client will ask us to fix up the grammar—change an expression such as "ain't" to something more proper. Usually, we edit the text a fair amount, but if "ain't" is a word a person habitually uses, we often encourage keeping it in to preserve the true voice. Because voice is so essential to our identity, especially within our families, changing someone's words to sound better grammatically sometimes strips the story of its original energy.

Ruth Ann Newby ("Reflections") speaks to "you," her family, in the form of a legacy letter that conveys the wisdom, patience, and good humor with which she has coped with her blindness. You get a sense of the woman through that voice, as she offers advice to her children and grandchildren.

Sometimes the subject's story is told in third person because that is the best or only way. Certainly it's the best voice when the person is deceased, overly modest, or not particularly good with words. Writing about her father in the third person allows Sally Steinberg in "Coffin Couture" to suggest her father's sense of style and whimsy, giving an account of his final party that captures his "fanciful way of being."

Several stories are based on memories of World War II and its aftermath. Sharon Waldman had never heard the story of how her father enlisted after the Japanese bombed Pearl Harbor ("The Sunday Our Lives Changed Forever") until she began interviewing him for a book about his life. His story captures the youthful idealism with which so many young men marched off to war.

Memories of trauma and hard times can be difficult for some to handle. Only with the passage of time are they able to begin processing and interpreting those memories; even then, they may not be ready to share their stories. Air Force veteran H.W. Smith recorded his life story on thirteen cassette tapes, which sat in a shoebox in his closet until his granddaughter Lisa Carpenter began transcribing them several years after his death. Just two of those thirteen tapes were about the war, and they referenced only its lighter side, including his story, "A Fair Hunt on Guadalcanal." According to Lisa, Smith spoke very little about the war while he was living and became agitated when others glamorized it. He told his grandchildren, "War is not pretty." Sometimes what's memorable in a personal history is what's not said.

John Maki hired Kitty Axelson-Berry's firm to interview him and transform those interviews into a narrative of his life, including his government service helping with the reconstruction of Japan after World War II. "A Nisei in Japan" combines a portion of an interview with excerpts from letters he wrote to his wife about the quality of life in Japan as he was experiencing it. Marek Stawiski's account of his family's wartime experiences in Warsaw places more emphasis on dramatic storytelling, with the help of Debra Moore.

Writing workshops are wonderful vehicles for getting people to write their own personal histories. For Ruta Sevo, an evening workshop provided memory- and emotion-provoking writing exercises. A sleepless night followed, but she arose the next morning with a sense of urgency and wrote "Ruta's Ethical Will." Reading it aloud later to her writing group stimulated others' memories and reflections and allowed Ruta to hear if it sounded the way she wanted it to sound. Sharing stories is as good a motivator for getting the stories told as any we've found.

Often personal historians are so busy helping clients tell their stories that they don't take time to tell their own. Recognizing no better motivation than a deadline and a receptive audience, many lead or participate in life-story writing or reminiscence groups. Such a group led Diane Dassow ("One Small Step") to relive in words the physical and emotional reality of being a small child in a bulky snow garment under an imperfect kindergarten system. Concrete and sensory details help convey how formidable school and clothing can seem to a small child and how much love a parent's patient attention to detail can convey.

A similar writing group encouraged Libby Atwater to write "A Worthwhile Search," the story of how and why, as an adopted woman, she sought and found her birth mother, and what she learned as a result. Personal history doesn't get much more personal than this, and the research requires more luck and courage than many of us might muster. Clearly, the emotions conveyed in this story will resonate for others wondering whether to search for their birth mother or birth child.

Sometimes our clients feel that a life story should be a rundown of all the rich and famous people they have met. Boasting and name-dropping are not enough, though; they must also share a story or an interesting observation. Pamela Daugavietis's story about an unexpected overnight visit by U. S. Representative Gerald Ford, and Leon Wilkinson's tale of a much-prepared-for but partly unscripted visit from President Ronald Reagan, show how discombobulating such an event can be for ordinary citizens, what it reveals about everyone involved, and how the afterglow from those brief encounters becomes part of the family history.

"Motown, Black and White" is an unusual celebrity story. It portrays musical artist Stevie Wonder as a teenager on the road with his white private tutor and road manager as the civil rights movement was heating up—a time when blacks and whites traveling together in the South was not quite forbidden, but not yet acceptable. The artful use of dialogue moves this inherently interesting story along while conveying the interaction between Stevie and his entourage.

Corporate histories that rise above the stereotype (dullness, fluff, or hype) do the same things good personal histories do. They tell several good stories within one good big story, they bring the main characters to life, and they provide history of interest beyond a specific boardroom. Greenhouse owners using coal year-round to sterilize their dirt is a detail that makes the Etna Supply Company come to life in Debra Moore's "The Legend of David Potgeter." And we remember Potgeter himself more vividly because we can picture his "hands like hams" and fingers so thick he had to use his pinky to dial the telephone.

Food stories are central to personal history. Sharon Waldman's "The Cake That Saved a College" shows how a recipe story told by her cousin easily became a personal history. You end up wanting to bake or taste that darned cake because you're curious about how offering a piece of it to Mr. Hardin actually changed the fate of a college. In a family heritage cookbook, the stories can provide much of the sizzle and many of the sweet touches.

Finally, we come to Willard Watson, whose story provides the words that became the title for our anthology— and believe us, we considered the grammatical reasons for changing "gonna" to "going to," but then the title lost its bounce. Although journalist Andrea Gross tells Willard's story in third person, notice how his voice and personality come through loud and clear. Andrea is part of the story, but only as a vehicle for conveying where Willard is in the physical world, what it's like to walk around in his world, and how Willard interacts with visitors from outside his personal spot on earth. When Willard concludes, "Now my words are gonna linger on, too," we smile with the recognition that he's speaking for everyone in this collection— indeed, everyone who undertakes a personal history.

This is a true story about my father's death.
It came to me when my family was thinking of
what to write in his obituary, since this small
incident captured his spirit and originality, and
his fanciful way of being. It also gives, at a
glance, an idea of many of the elements that
went into his life, from donuts to sailing to running to apparel—a kind of thumbnail sketch
hooked around the issue of what he would wear
in his coffin. He would have loved this story.

—Sally Steinberg

Coffin Couture

Sally Steinberg

On the day before his eightieth birthday, my father—
the King of Donuts, the man who took the machine
that made donuts to China—died of complications from
prostate cancer. He actually died of blue hands and feet, but
no doctor said that.

His father had invented the Wonderful Almost Human
Automatic Donut Machine, and together they had spread
donuts around the world. He had sailed the world in boats;
he had run its courses, winning a Silver Sneaker in the over-
sixty group. He also won a blue Surrey-with-Fringe-on-Top
in a raffle. It was an antique car he drove around town, collecting kids as he bumped down the streets. He got interested in flower arranging, studied Japanese ikebana, and made
flower creations that told stories—Moses and the Burning
Bush, the parting of the Red Sea.

During the months before his death, he planned his
eightieth birthday party. He had ordered two hundred fifty
balloons to be stationed at the entry to the retirement community where he lived, to flank the pastel ramps and halls,
cross his threshold, and deck his apartment.

The initial planning stages were spectacular. He created a menu—caviar, smoked salmon, champagne, cognac,
raspberry vacherin. Absolutely no vegetables. During the
summer, while his kids were away, he made repeated calls
for shrimp, for birds-of-paradise, for caviar, for the balloons.

He was totally bedridden, maintained with a morphine
pump inserted surgically into his insides, and with boxes of

pills for this and that, and pills to counter the bad effects of other pills.

He gave his wife trouble when she said a pianist would be too expensive and when she cut the number of balloons. Nonetheless, he was so devoted to her that he commissioned his twin sister to buy her a diamond ring for his birthday. Lacking funds, he settled for the idea of paste jewels.

The Donut King, in his Pucci jacket

Years before, he had told his kids he did not want to be buried in a blue suit. "Put me in my Pucci jacket," he had said.

The Pucci was a velvet number in a bold, busy, colorful print. All his life, he had been a flamboyant dresser. He wore leopard bikinis and ruffled shirts, a fire-engine red jacket from Sicily with embroidered lapels, and a long maroon caftan braided with gold.

The day before his birthday, he started to turn blue. Nobody believed he wouldn't make it. At 3:30 a.m., after rattling and scratching for breath, he stopped breathing for good.

The idea of the jacket met with resistance, but we got it out and hung it in the living room. The funeral director looked at it and lit up, a twinkle in his eye.

That day, the Donut King turned slowly to wax in his bed. We all wanted to be with him to say goodbye and so kept the heavy men in dark glasses from taking him on the stretcher and zipping him into the bag. Finally, they did. And they took the jacket away with him

The next day, in his room, we laid tables, got balloons, and had his party. We read things about him, sang a song he had asked for, and ate the shrimp he had ordered. We stood near his birds-of-paradise, in the place where the hospital mask and oxygen tank had been the day before. We had his favorite raspberry meringue cake with candles. We sang "Happy Birthday" and blew out the candles. And we saw the star he looked at every night out the window.

I wondered about the timing of my father's death, remembering that he had a taste for the sensational. He loved what he called "putting things over." What person dies one day and is reborn the next? I could see him winking.

The next day, on what would have been the first day of his eighty-first year, his funeral was held.

There he was in his Pucci jacket. There he was, dressed for a party. There he was… in his Pucci jacket, forever.

The following vignette is from the oral history of Catherine Munson, who grew up in the Dust Bowl during the Depression and is now a prominent real estate developer and philanthropist in Marin County, California. Many times in her life, she has found herself in unlikely and thrilling circumstances, always by a fluke. Catherine describes in this story how she solved a murder mystery at the age of six, quite by accident. "I wasn't trying to be Nancy Drew," she laughs. "I hadn't started to read her books yet. I was just <u>there</u>!"

—Trena Cleland

Sand Hills Murder Mystery

Catherine Munson, Narrator

I was born in 1928 and grew up in Albion, Nebraska, a tiny little town of about 1,200 at the end of the railroad spur. Immediately beyond the town, the Sand Hills began. To this day, they are not very populated, and the train still turns around when it gets to Albion. There's no need for it to go into the Sand Hills.

It was the height of the Great Depression, and my father was basically unemployed. A certified public accountant, he once owned the local Chevrolet agency, which had long since gone down the tubes. But when I was a child, he ran a bicycle shop. He would come home at night and put the change from his pocket on the table. That was the family income. It might be fifty-four cents; it might be seventy-nine cents for the day.

The Depression was the constant talk of the town, but as a child, I really found it boring. I couldn't see that we were in the worst of dire straits. We were in straits, all right, but I didn't think it was all that bad. Our parents may have been traumatized; we children weren't.

The dust storms, though, were frightening, terrifying. They were dirty and nasty, and they ruined our crops. I was interested in the crops around us and passionate about the weather. We prayed for rain. Except that whenever we got it, it was usually too much, and we had torrential floods.

I had a lot of freedom to roam. I was no more than six, maybe five, when I bought a bicycle with the seven dollars I had earned by selling string beans from our garden door-to-door. It was a great boy's bike, which I painted raspberry, and it transported me wherever I wanted to go.

The little Carnegie Library was about two blocks from our house. There were limited things to do in Albion, so I'd go to the library and check out a book or stay there and read for twenty or thirty minutes. Then I'd get on my bike and go some other place. Although I read quickly and read a lot, I didn't hang around the library. I went there because I had my route with my bike, and it was simply one more place to stop. Madge Graden, the librarian, was a friend of my mother, and she put up with me. We had a casual "hello, good-bye" relationship.

I was six when my father came home from the bicycle shop one day and said, "Sheriff Smoyer is missing." Smoyer was Albion's sheriff. My father was a deputy sheriff, one of

Sand Hills near Catherine Munson's childhood home in Albion, Nebraska

the few paying jobs for local able-bodied men in those days. Everybody was very concerned, and the deputies all fanned out to look for the sheriff.

The next day, I went out on my bike, just making the rounds. Albion was a little town; it didn't take very long to make the rounds. I went into the library, read a little, and came back out. Three men and two women were sitting on the lawn. To my eyes, they were certainly adults, but they were probably in their twenties. I didn't know them and thought, *They don't belong on the grass.* So I went up to them and said, "You mustn't sit on the lawn because Madge Graden will be mad at you if she finds out that you're sitting here."

"Oh, yeah, really?"

"Yes, you really mustn't sit on this grass. You should get up and go someplace else." That was the extent of my concern—to get them off Madge Graden's grass.

After leaving the library, I heard the noon whistle and went home. The whole town lived by the noon whistle, which reminded us to go home for dinner, and the five o'clock whistle, our signal to go home for supper.

At dinner, my father was very upset because they couldn't find Sheriff Smoyer or his car. It had been about eighteen hours since he disappeared. It was our custom during dinner to listen to the radio station out of Norfolk, which was about a hundred miles away. The noon news was broadcast by Don Bridge, the "Hootmahn." A Scottish fellow, he was always offering prizes for all kinds of trivial things. In those days, any prize—even one box of Cracker Jacks popcorn—was a big deal.

The Hootmahn announced that they couldn't find Sheriff Smoyer in Albion, Nebraska. "Everyone should be on the lookout," he said and described some possible suspects in the sheriff's disappearance.

I was sitting at the table, eating my mashed potatoes and gravy. My ears perked right up. I told Dad, "Those are the people that were on Madge Graden's grass! That's exactly who they were!"

"Oh, my God," he said.

Dad immediately called the sheriff's office. Then we called the Hootmahn in Norfolk. That was a big deal because it was a long distance telephone call. On the air, I told Don about the people I had seen and described what they were wearing in a little more detail. I could hear myself on the radio, talking with him!

Well, by golly, they apprehended those young people in the Sand Hills three or four days later, and they had indeed murdered Sheriff Smoyer.

Oh, I was a hero to Don Bridge, the Hootmahn. And to think, I even won a deck of playing cards as a prize! Can you stand it? What more could you ask? I don't know why they murdered the sheriff. My own excitement in identifying the killers was as far as I went!

Every American who was around on Sunday, December 7, 1941, seems to recall where they were and how they heard the news that the Japanese had attacked Pearl Harbor, crippling the Pacific fleet and killing 2,335 servicemen and 68 civilians. My father remembered where he was and what happened the next day. I never heard the story before interviewing him for a book about his life. The image of the crowd at the Enlistment Center in downtown Dallas on Monday, December 8, 1941, is one I'll never forget, and is now part of his book, The Adventures of Monty I. in the 20th Century *(2006).*

—Sharon Levine Waldman

The Sunday Our Lives Changed forever

Monty I. Levine, Narrator

I met Raymond "Tailspin" Bales in 1941 when we both worked at North American Aviation in Dallas, testing the airplanes they built. Tailspin and I became good friends, and after he took me out to his farm to meet his folks, Mama and Pop Bales, they became like a second family to me.

One Sunday, Pop Bales, Tailspin, and I went rabbit hunting. Pop Bales had a shotgun, I had a .22 rifle, and Tailspin had a pistol. We went way out in the brush, tromping and jumping over ravines, looking for rabbits for Mama Bales to cook for rabbit stew.

In the distance, we heard a noise. Every farmhouse had a triangle [dinner bell] that the mother would "ding, ding, ding" to tell you it's time to eat. But when it went "ding-ding-ding-ding-ding-ding" [rapidly], something was happening. Could be a fire. *Mama's in trouble!*

We started running, jumping streams and gulleys. When I broke out of the underbrush and into the clearing, I could see Mama in the distance, looking for us and waving her apron.

"What happened, Mama?" I gasped, running to her.

"It just came over the radio," she said as Tailspin and Pop arrived. "The Japanese have attacked Pearl Harbor. Thousands of our men are dead. They practically wiped out our Navy."

Now, I didn't know where Pearl Harbor was; most people didn't. But we knew that a lot of big Navy ships were knocked out, and we knew that when you kill a thousand Americans, we're going to do something about it. We were going to get in a fight with Japan, and it was going to be a toughie.

What went wrong? We didn't know. But we knew that our lives were changed forever.

After Tailspin and I went back to our apartment that night, we got a call from the chief test pilot for North American Aviation. "There's going to be a war. Everybody is frozen at their jobs. We need to get these planes out as quickly as we can."

I told Tailspin, "I don't care what the Chief says. I'm not about to stay testing airplanes when there's a big fight going on." He disagreed, but I wanted to be in the middle of it. I was twenty-two years old and gung-ho.

The day after Pearl Harbor was attacked, the president and Congress declared war on Japan. I called in sick and drove to the Enlistment Center at the Post Office in downtown Dallas at seven o'clock that morning.

My God! A line of men already stretched from the door leading into the post office, down the steps, all the way around the block, crossing the street to the next block. And they were still coming in from all over. There was no room to park because there were horses tied up at the parking meters. Guys had been riding in from ranches all night to sign up and fight. Some of them had six-guns strapped to their waists, old-time gunfighter style. Some guys were in full dress clothes like office workers. They were all talking and socializing. There were no barriers; we were all Americans—black and brown and white. Religion or race didn't matter. As Americans, we were undaunted...The Japanese were against us, and we were against them. What supreme confidence we had. Of course, we were going to whip their asses!

I went up to the officer standing at the door and said, "Corporal, I've already got a pilot's license, and I work out at North American, but I want to go into combat."

"We need guys like you," he said. "Come right in."

The sergeant inside signed me in and asked, "What is the name on your birth certificate?"

"Monroe Irving Levine."

He started to type.

"Hold it! My name is not Monroe, it's Monty."

Monty Levine, a test pilot in Dallas, Texas—before December 7, 1941

"I'm sorry, sir, but we've got to sign you in as it is on your birth certificate," he said.

"Sergeant, I've been known as Monty for years. And if I get in the regular Army, I want to be called Monty."

"Just a minute, sir. I'll have to talk to the Captain." He went to an office door with a frosted glass panel. In those days, there was no air conditioning, but the frosted glass came up to within three feet of the ceiling so you'd get a flow of air. So I could hear a voice in that office, talking on the telephone in a state of panic..."Yeah, but you don't know where they're gonna hit next! We're gonna have to get 'em. We can't let 'em land in America!"

The sergeant knocked on the door. "Captain?"

"**What is it?!**" the captain yelled.

"There's a guy out here. He's already a pilot, and he wants to come in as Monty, but his real name on his birth certificate is Monroe—"

"Sergeant, goddamn it, we just lost a thousand men! The Japanese could be coming here! What the hell do I care what you call him? Call him anything you want! Sign him up! Get him in!"

So I went in as Monty.

I called North American and told the chief, "I'll tell you where to send my last check, but I quit. I'm going into combat."

The Chief said, "You can't do that. You've already got prior instructions. You're frozen in the job."

"I'm not frozen anywhere. I'm following my latest instructions, and that's to go to Houston, Ellington Field, and train for combat."

I was on my way.

H.W. Smith was my grandfather. As a child, I often lived with him or next door to him. Over time, he recorded his life story on thirteen cassette tapes, which were placed in a shoebox and virtually forgotten following his death in 1996. While trying to come up with Christmas ideas for my family in 2004, I suddenly remembered the tapes and realized what great gifts his stories would be for all of us. Each year now, I transcribe stories from those old tapes and create CDs for my family. They treasure them. This is one of those stories.

—Lisa Carpenter

A Fair Hunt on Guadalcanal

H. W. Smith, Narrator

During World War II, I served in the Seabees on a Navy attack transport. A few days out from the island of Espiritu, we arrived off the beach at Guadalcanal. A contingent of Marines—the first Marine Raiders, an elite unit established to conduct amphibious infantry warfare—hit the shore first. There was a little light rifle fire and the burst of a machine-gunner or "B-A-R" (Browning automatic rifle). As the Marines went into the jungle, we came ashore on their heels. Our chore, if we didn't have to fight, was to hit the beach and immediately unload supplies before the Japanese could come and sink the ship.

*H.W. Smith (inset and second from left, back row) with his Seabees
heavy equipment crew on Guadalcanal, circa 1942*

For the next fifty-four hours, we worked, and we
worked, and we worked. When we finally were told, "That
is your last boat," I managed to stagger over to the shade of
a palm tree and flop down.

The sun was scorching when I woke up. Burning up, I
crawled back over into the shade and didn't wake again
until sometime in the wee hours of the morning. Do you
have any idea how cold it can get on the beach of a tropical
island at night? That sweat chill just soaks through your bones.

My Seabee outfit got things organized. Though I had
planned to be home because I was sure the war would be
over, I ate my Christmas dinner on the shore of Guadalcanal
on December 28, 1942—my wedding anniversary.

During this same time, my wife, Skip, had gone to work
for Patterson Overall Factory in Miami, Oklahoma. But
when she found that Douglas Aircraft out of Tulsa paid better, she went to Tulsa to earn a living. Of course, she earned
more than I did. She built airplane parts and did more for

the war effort in that job than I did, even though I was on the front lines. Without all those people back home putting all that material together, there was no way we could have won even the smallest skirmish.

We had been ashore just a few days when we moved inland to clear the brush and build our camp. Well, the Japanese found out we were there, and they sent a bombing raid over. It was the first time I ever heard bombs. Nobody had to tell me what they were. The bombs were falling here, thither, and yon around us. The Japanese bombers seemed to be bombing the entire area because they couldn't see where we were at night. Sticks of bombs were coming down, but we didn't have time to dig any bomb shelters or foxholes or anything else for protection. All we could do was lie on the ground and hope the bombs missed us.

I know now that this one stick that was coming down held five bombs. The first one hit. Then the second one hit, in line with where the first one hit and where I was lying. The third one hit, and it was still in line. By the time the fourth bomb hit, I knew that fifth one was going to land in my hip pocket. I knew I was dead. No, my life didn't flash before my eyes and all that kind of stuff like the writers say it does. The only thing that came through my mind was... "Lord, please take care of Skip." Now, you are not supposed to make fun and games of serious and religious things, I guess. However, that bomb landed close! It jarred my kinfolks in the old country. I mean that ground came up and slammed me up out of it and then dropped me back into it. I hurt, but I hadn't been hit. The bomb dropped short. I am not going to say that I wasn't scared. I was terrified! Anybody who isn't scared in combat is a complete idiot.

One day on Guadalcanal, I decided I would like to eat some meat—something other than the usual worms in my oatmeal. So I went hog hunting. Though we were not supposed to take any of the food the natives depended on, I had seen some really nice plump hogs in the area. Off I went into the jungle, snooping around for something to kill. Sure enough, I heard a grunt and squatted down to see through the brush and have a fair field of vision. About 30 yards away stood a big ol' black hog, a wild boar. His tusks were nearly 5 inches long and stuck up alongside his jaw, but I wasn't paying much attention to that at the time.

I put my rifle up and shot that bugger right between the eyes. That knocked him back on his haunches a bit. I slapped another round in the chamber as he was coming my way. Again, I hit him right between the eyes. That second bullet made him pause only momentarily. As he continued to come toward me, I slapped the bolt again and shot the animal a third time. Well, he kind of paused again. I fanned the bolt one more time and shot a fourth time. At that point, he was about 30 feet away and coming up fast. I don't think he really had my welfare in mind. Not touching the bolt this time, I dropped the rifle and turned to shinny up the nearest tree. Finally, that boar went down. Its heavy body slid to within 10 or 15 feet of me before stopping.

Eventually, I climbed down and poked the hog to see if he was dead. Then I inspected the bugger to see why he hadn't gone down the first time I shot him. One bullet (the fourth one, I'm sure) had gone right down his spinal column and shattered his neck bone. All four bullet holes were located between the animal's eyes and could have been covered with a silver dollar. Three of those bullets, however, had traveled through his muscles, and one was lodged in his hip. Peeling the one damaged ham away from the hip all the way around his rump, I opened him up and stripped out the tenderloins. Would you believe… By the time I had lifted those ham and tenderloins onto one shoulder and my rifle over the other shoulder, that was all I wanted to carry. He was a purty fair-sized hunk of hog.

As I came out of the jungle by the river, I met a couple of the native boys who worked on the airfield. They were tame fellows, so I wasn't scared of them. Using sign language, I finally got it across that they would find the remains of that hog if they followed my tracks. For my money, it was theirs.

Back at camp, I took the ham and tenderloins to the cook shack. The cook said he would fix it for me but wanted half the meat. I got the shank end half of the ham back. We had pork that afternoon; we had pork that night in my tent with a couple of neighbors. The next morning, we didn't eat wormy oatmeal for breakfast. We ate pork, or I should say ham. Needless to say, no pork was left for lunch. But we sure had stuffed ourselves for a while.

The day after my hunting spree, I passed the natives' camp. They had a spit set up with a three-legged hog on it. The fire they had built under that old bugger had charred the outside, but the inside was as raw as if that hog was still alive. In fact, it took them about three days to cook him thoroughly. So maybe it wasn't too bad that I did the hunting and shared with the natives.

In 2002, John M. Maki hired our company to interview him and transform the taped interviews into a written narrative. His story was unique. A nisei (born in America of Japanese immigrants), he worked for the U.S. government in the reconstruction of Japan after World War II. Mr. Maki was ninety-four years old when we met him. He suffered a heart attack the following year but later resumed work on his memoir project. At the age of ninety-six, he finally saw his 280-page narrative in print. He passed away December 7, 2006. The following story is an excerpt from his book, Voyage Through the Twenty-First Century, *based on interviews conducted by staff writer Alison de Groot and freelancer John Bowman.*

—Kitty Axelson-Berry

A Nisei in Japan

John M. Maki, Narrator

As part of Washington's response to the Whitney Memorandum, five or ten of us left Washington by plane on January 30, 1946, and arrived in Tokyo on February 22 after being stuck at Hamilton Field outside San Francisco for a week and Hickam Field in Honolulu for ten days. The reason we were delayed for so long was simple… There were numerous planes, pilots, and passengers, but because of demobilization there was no one to service the planes. Meanwhile, the momentous drafting of the MacArthur version of Japan's new constitution was taking place in Tokyo. It is one of the major disappointments of my life that I was not a part of that. But I survived.

A rather amusing thing happened after we landed at Atsugi Airfield, about twenty miles from Tokyo. It was dusk, and we boarded an Army bus for Tokyo. On the bus (he may have been on our flight, too) was a well-known American football coach on a morale mission to talk to the troops. The bus made several stops to drop off passengers, and the coach got off at one of them. We heard his voice, which was very loud, say roughly this: "Well, take a look at that—a GI with a little Jap girl. We're going to have to put a stop to that." It took only a few days to recognize what an impossible job it was going to be to put a stop to that.

Japan was in a real mess as a result of months of intensive bombing before the end of the war. I had expected to see defeated people, people suffering from lack of housing, food, and supplies—people who had just lost a war and were experiencing the first military occupation in their country's history. But I had been there not more than a day before I noticed something completely different. Everybody, meaning the Japanese civilians, seemed to be doing something, and what they were doing was trying to survive. They were not just living in defeat but were going about their daily lives as if life was worth living. I speedily came to the conclusion that Japan would get over the war fairly rapidly. Nothing I saw during my six months there indicated that this impression was wrong.

It can be argued, and it's probably true, that the only people I saw were those capable of that kind of activity and that others were silently suffering. The amount of destruction was almost unbelievable. The United States Strategic Bombing Survey was carrying on an intensive investigation of the bombings' impact. One of their striking statistics was that, on average, about 50 percent of every Japanese city had been leveled. That was certainly true of Tokyo.

I had been curious during the war about how the Japanese central government operated. With part of the mission of Government Section being to oversee "the political reorientation of Japan" (among other things, the reorganization of the Japanese central government), I decided to draw up a proposal outlining the importance of learning how the Japanese government was operating in the midst of the devastation. That proposed study became my principal task for the six months I was with the occupation.

I was the only staff member in Government Section to work on this project. Nisei in the U.S. Army were assigned to translate and interpret for me. Although I could follow a conversation, I was by no means fluent in Japanese. I gathered material in a number of areas, including the actual setup and management of the Japanese government ministries. Again, this was in a ruined Tokyo. I collected information about how the government managed to function with few automobiles and telephones. One large ministry, for instance, had only 120 telephones.

John M. Maki, circa 1930

One of my more interesting assignments was on April 10, 1946, at Kyushu, the southernmost main island. I monitored the first "normal" election in Japan. Although Japan had a history of general elections as far back as 1890, they had been organized, supervised, and monitored by the government and were not free. My assignment was to monitor the election in Kyushu and write a report on the way it was run.

I would like to round out this chapter in my life by introducing some of the letters I wrote to my wife, Mary. When I left her behind in Washington, I made up my mind to write every day. We ended up with about 185 letters from the time of my departure from Hamilton Field to my homecoming on a military transport from Yokohama to Seattle. (My return trip took only ten days, whereas before the war, the same voyage took fourteen days on a Japanese ship). The following are excerpts from those letters, indicating some of my observations and reactions to the Japan I saw at that time.

March 23, 1946

Now I'll tell you about some of the things that my friend Nakai-obasan told me about life in Tokyo today—against the background of her comment that the yen today is worth about what a yen was worth when we were here in 1936. [In 2008, the average value of the yen is about one cent, whereas the value in 1946 was approximately fifty cents.]

1. They can get a bath once every ten days.

2. A bunch of spinach costs about Y8, when you can get it.

3. People are fairly well fed now because it is possible to get stuff on the black market at terrific prices. But what will happen after money disappears from pockets, nobody knows.

4. The rice ration is the equivalent of about six bowls a day, but it does not always appear in the form of rice. Sometimes they are given rice equivalents such as sweet potatoes, wheat, and bread.

5. She showed me the new bread. It is dark and firm-textured. They are given two small loaves, weighing about a pound. She said that Uncle Ojisan had eaten half a loaf for breakfast and taken the other half with him for lunch. A pound of black market butter costs Y150.

6. She says they never get a charcoal distribution. They use coal, charred wood, and something resembling charcoal that they pick up or buy from others who pick it up. In 1944, the charcoal ration was two bundles for the year.

7. They never have sugar anymore.

Kurume, April 10, 1946

Today was the Big Day, the first peacetime election. Two officers and I went to a little village called Emi. The polling place was in the local school. There was a line of 300 or 400 people, almost all women—young, old, and middle-aged. Some had babies on their backs. Some looked quite stupid; others not.

It was easy to be very cynical or very optimistic. The cynical would say that these women were just a herd—that they were told to vote—and that is what they were doing without knowing what they were doing. The optimistic could say that here was the dawn of a new era in Japan. I was cynical, but I was also thrilled by the sight of a little old woman, bent double as so many of them are, hobbling up to the ballot box and dropping in her vote. The efficiency, the seriousness, and the earnestness of the occasion were very impressive.

En route back to Tokyo, April 12, 1946

We passed through Hiroshima around 11 o'clock. We couldn't see the main area of devastation from the train. What we did see wasn't much different from other cities except for the trees. They stood black and dead with their branches burned short, like burned skeletons. At the same time, their movements were the only sign of life on August 6, 1945 (the date the atomic bomb was dropped on Hiroshima). It was more like a warning. It was not a thrilling sight. Neither was it frightening. Here was physical devastation wrought by man, which proved that he does not yet have the moral sense he needs to survive. These are not things I've just been thinking about now, but what ran through my mind as I was watching those trees.

The first time I taught a workshop on "How to Write an Ethical Will," one of the participants was Ruta Sevo, a former client from the National Science Foundation, for whom I had written a book about what NSF researchers had learned about girls and science. Ruta had just retired and had signed up for the course on a lark—she was starting her creative period. During our first weekly class, I asked everyone to write their obituary and then gave them a couple more writing exercises. By the end of the evening, they all seemed to be undergoing an unwilling life review. (I've since learned to introduce things a bit more gradually.) The next week, Ruta told us that she had trouble sleeping after the first workshop, but she got up the next morning and started writing, the words just pouring from her. She felt good about the result, which she wrote partly for her nieces and nephews. "I signed up for your course thinking I would write a parody of it," she explained, "but then I realized it was real!"

—Pat McNees

Ruta's Ethical Will

Ruta Sevo

To those who are able to read this… Thank you. One of the major themes in my life was to connect with people. Why did I write this? Because I believe that we all serve a purpose in each other's lives, and this might help you figure out what we had to do for each other.

I was born a refugee on the last day of World War II in Europe, a day of global celebration. A Lithuanian psychic once told me that my first four years explain more about my life than any fifty or more that followed.

My parents had fled Lithuania with the German occupiers to leave behind the returning Russian occupiers. Imagine the grief of leaving your family and home behind, risking your life to steal potatoes, carrying one baby in a buggy and one on the way. Imagine being traumatized by the German death squads who took your friends away in the night and shot hundreds in the woods. Your family was on the list the Russians kept, of those to be deported to a slow, cold, hungry death in Siberia once they got back into Lithuania. The country, the size of West Virginia, had no defenses. The small percentage of educated urban population mixed collaborators and victims, all neighbors. Imagine Bosnia and Rwanda. Neighbors killing neighbors, everyone scrounging for food, forced to take a side and watch out for themselves if they could.

Thanks to America, my parents escaped to a new country. They had to forget the past and grab any job, regardless

*Ruta Sevo (bottom right) as a refugee immigrating to United States
at age four, with her father, Eric Pempe, mother, Sophie,
and brother Saulius (circa 1949)*

of their status and education before. Thanks to their education, they knew enough English to start. They had to learn how to get a job and how to get ahead. They had two children to feed, and soon three and four and five. They had no friends and could not communicate with family in Lithuania for the next forty-five years. I never knew my grandparents.

I did not appreciate their situation for decades of my life. My immature self was resentful for the lack of attention, the cloud of sadness and depression, the cold authority, and the social isolation of the early years. My parents were not trusting and did not learn from friends and neighbors, or seek out advice. They were very sad and tired. My older brother (by one and a half years) and I fought to the point that we did not speak through my teen years, and nobody knew what to do about it. My parents sponsored a man from Germany who went wild with exuberance in America, drinking and carousing. He died quickly in a car accident. They adopted my youngest brother, who arrived as a four-year-old emotional wreck. This was their first fifteen years in America.

I wanted a great deal—to see the world, to read everything, and to live fully. I could not have a great deal.

On top of my family's situation was my encounter with bias against girls. Almost as soon as I decided I wanted to be Albert Schweitzer (doctor, humanitarian, writer, musician, and African missionary) or a nuclear physicist, I was told by counselors and nearly everyone else: "Girls cannot do that." My parents were absent, or just fearful and constraining. At the same time as my view of the world grew large, the messages of limitation grew loud and clear. I became very depressed for all that I could not have. And grateful for any good thing that I could have—Girl Scout camps and trips, family outdoor vacations, books from the library, my baby brother Pete (the only one with whom I had a hugging relationship).

My early struggle was about scaling my ambitions and wishes to whatever I thought might be accessible to me, without a lot of adult help. I cry now when I hear about mentoring programs, especially for immigrants. That would have helped a lot. I was very fearful of poverty—the bag lady scenario, because it meant being a bored, tired, lonely victim exploited by the meanest elements in society.

I have been extremely lucky, nevertheless. Lucky to be

in America, lucky to have my strong, resourceful, competent, and risk-taking parents, lucky to go to college, lucky to spend a year abroad in Germany, and lucky to fall in love with or befriend people who explained "how things work" to me. I was lucky to get a federal fellowship that paid for my entire Ph.D., including fieldwork in India, even though the university was biased against women and the degree in a narrow, low-demand field yielded no job. The degree was my ticket to more support from what felt like a hostile world, as I earned another degree fairly easily. Then the jobs opened up, with my first job at age thirty-two. Every job I had was a dream come true, for fun and for money. My hunger for life and the world, and my encounters with discrimination against women, led me through five careers.

I didn't have children because I did not trust any man to support me financially through age thirty-five. Everything I saw around me, especially some poignant movies of the 1960s and 1970s, indicated that women (especially unmarried or divorced) with children basically selected themselves out of society. They supposedly would be punished, shunned, ostracized, and underpaid the rest of their lives. I discovered through experience and by reading sociology literature much later that this was not far from true. Having a child was intellectual and social/economic suicide. I would have been Sylvia Plath without the published novels.

One of my life lessons is that children do not appreciate their parents as people. I tried to make up for my decades of escape from my family—escape from problems I could not grasp or solve. I gained deep respect for the sacrifice and challenge of raising me. My parents had dreams, too, and look what happened. I gained empathy for my brothers, who had to navigate their own dreams from this base, good and bad.

My history explains a lot of things. How much I love and appreciate what I got and the fact that I was alive and well and had fabulous friendships and a real and adopted extended family of love and respect. I am impatient with those who drain the spirit or resources of others, to be lazy or indulgent. I expect people to pull themselves together more than they might be capable. My history also explains why I fiercely looked out for myself financially, why I built skills and consumed information about "things" so I would be equipped for a wide range of problems in life. Why I did not stay in unhappy relationships, or trade or compromise my ambitions or chances for a decent livelihood for romance and sex. I lived in an unfriendly world, near poverty, for my first thirty years. Independence was survival and freedom.

My history also explains why I am so grateful to Jeff, my late-life partner, for bringing me the happiness of a lifetime. I am grateful I lived long enough to get wise enough to be there when he showed up, to complete me to where I felt I had everything.

I did not become Albert Schweitzer, but I hope I became a good mentor, friend, and lover. I feel that I finally got everything. I gave back in hundreds of small ways. I had hoped to give back in a bigger, more public way, but my ideas may have exceeded my talent and skills. Still, I feel that I made a difference one-on-one many, many times, especially with women whom I met through my job at the National Science Foundation when I was an official moneygiver (with others reviewing my recommendations, of course.)

I hope that your life is closer to a perfect life from start to finish—loving, trusting, sharing, fun, stimulating, adventurous, creative, aesthetic, solvent, secure, giving. We try.

I am not leaving you. As a spiritualist, I believe I am looking over your shoulder as you hear this or read it. You can talk to me. You might hear me talk back. As a Buddhist, I believe I am coming back to learn from some of you again, as souls in my radius. Death is a transition and a milestone of achievement; it marks the completion of one of many cycles. It is a celebration, because there is divine respite between cycles.

You and I had a reason for meeting, I believe. You gave me something I needed in order to grow, whether it was support or friendship or love or a challenge. The challenges are no fun but yield growth, which is a ticket to wisdom. Think of what you did for me, and feel me pat you on the back. I love you for it.

A few years ago, I was sitting on my dermatologist's examining table, shirt pulled over my head, so Dr. Stawiski could remove a few moles from my back. As he worked, the doctor asked in his heavy Polish accent, "So, Debbie, what have you been up to?" I spoke into my shirt and explained that I was helping people write their memoirs. "Send me some information on that," he said upon leaving the examining room. I did, and Dr. Stawiski hired me to write his life story. This is the dramatic beginning of that story.

—Debra Moore

From the Ashes of Warsaw

Marek A. Stawiski, M.D., Narrator

My mother, Irena Meyer, was born in Poland in 1915 during World War I, while her family was running east, away from the Germans. I don't quite understand this because her father was half German. I know they almost perished from hunger. They returned sometime later to Poland, and my mother was raised in Lodz. She earned her dental degree at the University of Warsaw around 1938, right before the second World War.

She met my father, Felix Stawiski, when a wealthy girlfriend invited her to her farm, and he was also at the gathering. Felix was six years older than Irena and had earned his law degree from the University of Warsaw. He was her first boyfriend, and she fell deeply in love with him. Felix, as they say, liked women. Irena was a beautiful woman. They married in 1943, and I was born in Warsaw on May 10, 1944—turbulent times in that city's history.

Warsaw was traditionally home to the Polish intelligentsia—professors, doctors, military leaders, and intellectuals. At the start of World War II, in September 1939, the Germans took control of the city. By November, the Nazis issued decrees intended to control and oppress the Jews, including an order forcing all Jews over the age of twelve to identify themselves by wearing a Star of David on their sleeve. During the summer of 1942, about 300,000 Jews were sent from Warsaw to the death camp at Treblinka. The Jewish Resistance successfully fought against the Germans for twenty days in the spring of 1943 in what was called the Warsaw Ghetto Uprising. The Germans eventually crushed the revolt and captured 56,000 Jews, shooting thousands and sending the others to concentration camps. This event was well portrayed in the 2002 film *The Pianist*.

Without warning, the Gestapo would round up Poles by blocking a street from both ends with their cars, trapping everybody in between. Then the officers would take their prisoners to Gestapo Police Headquarters, where it was decided who to shoot and who to send to concentration camps. My father was caught in one of those traps. A compulsive guy, he carried a notebook with hundreds of addresses in his jacket pocket. Although he was not a Jew, the authorities felt he might be connected somehow with the Polish Underground, and it looked as if they might send him to a concentration camp. My beautiful, blonde mother took all the gold jewelry she had and went to the Gestapo. She smiled at the men, and they liked her. The officer in charge had two choices—he could take the gold and shoot her because she was trying to bribe him, or he could take the gold and let my father go. Thankfully, he did the latter. I think Mother was pregnant with me at the time.

I was just a few months old when the Russian Army approached Warsaw from the east and camped on the other side of the Vistula River. They encouraged the Polish Home Army to expel the Germans from the city and promised to act as backup. On August 1, 1944, the Polish fighters attacked the Germans and kept them at bay for thirty days. The Soviets never came to the aid of the Poles, however. They also refused to let in American and British ammunition and relief supplies. It was in Stalin's interest to destroy the entire Polish intelligentsia, for it would then be far easier for him to control the peasants and the workers.

According to my mother, there was a great deal of bombardment as the Russian troops approached Warsaw that summer. Following one of the bombardments, a Russian spy came to inspect and to report on the state of the city. While there, he developed an acute toothache and came to my mother, a dentist, for help. She extracted his tooth. He didn't have money to pay her but said that he would give her an important secret instead. The Russian advised her to take me and whatever she could carry and leave Warsaw the next day because the fighting would soon erupt. Mother got a horse and buggy, and took me south about two hundred miles to Krakow. She left behind my nanny, Posia, as well as my father, who would not leave because he was so independent.

Within a week or so, the worst uprising yet broke out in Warsaw. My father decided to run, realizing that if he stayed, he would be a hero but would die. He ran through the sewers and escaped Warsaw. The German troops destroyed the ghetto and killed about 200,000 Poles—all the children and almost all the women. Those who didn't die were sent on trains to the concentration camp at Auschwitz.

By October 2, the Polish Resistance was completely crushed, but the Germans were extremely angry with all Poles for the uprising. In retaliation, they razed 85 percent of the city and deported what few people were left. My birthplace was destroyed.

Although Posia, my sixty-year-old nanny, didn't resist the soldiers, they still arrested her and put her on a train bound for Auschwitz. When the train made a stop, she just got off and walked into a field. The Nazis shot at her but apparently decided to let her go because she was an old lady. With only rotten potatoes that she found in the fields for nourishment, Posia walked for two weeks before finding my mother and me. It would be another six months before my father joined us.

Thus, my family was reunited in Krakow and survived the war.

This selection is a chapter from my memoir, Coming Home to Myself. *It is the story of the night a congressman from Michigan stayed in our northern Michigan home, just three months before he became vice president of the United States and less than a year before he became president.*

—*Pamela H. Daugavietis*

A Surprise Overnight Guest

Pamela H. Daugavietis

On September 22, 1973, the dining room at Stafford's Bay View Inn in Petoskey, Michigan, was filled to capacity. It was Jack's twenty-ninth birthday, but the one hundred fifty Republican Party faithful who paid to attend didn't come for cake and ice cream. They came to hear Gerald R. Ford, popular congressman from Michigan's 5th Congressional District since 1948 and minority leader of the U.S. House of Representatives since 1965.

As Emmet County Republican Party Chairman, Jack had arranged the fundraising dinner and invited Congressman Ford, whom we had never met, to speak. The congressman was seated on Jack's left at the head table. I was on Jack's right. As we finished our meal, Jack turned to Mr. Ford and said, "We have a room for you at the Holiday Inn south of town, but if you want to stay with us, you can get an extra hour of sleep. We live north of here and closer to the airport. Your plane leaves at 6:00 a.m."

I couldn't believe my ears. Jack hadn't mentioned his intentions to me. I was even more surprised when I heard Mr. Ford say, "Why, that's very kind of you."

Jack's parents lived in Columbus, Ohio, but were here for his birthday. Fortunately, they were staying in Indian River. Otherwise, our tiny 1,200-square-foot chalet in the woods couldn't have accommodated another overnight guest. Jack had left early to meet Congressman Ford at the airport. I came with Jack's parents, who were seated several tables away. Excusing myself, I went over to tell them of the change in plans.

"Jack just invited Gerald Ford to spend the night with us, and Mr. Ford accepted," I whispered. "The house is a mess. I need to go home right away. Can you take me?"

Hurrying back to the head table, I told Jack that his parents and I were leaving, just as the staff started serving dessert and coffee.

When we got home, the boys were sound asleep—Bobby, sixteen months old, in his crib in the tiny bedroom upstairs, and John, three, across from Bobby's room in the loft that was open to the living room below.

Jack's dad drove the babysitter home while his mother and I got busy. We took John out of the double bed in the loft and put him in our bed downstairs. The sheets on the upstairs bed where Mr. Ford would sleep needed changing. We only had one other set of linens—clean but worn and faded. I prayed Mr. Ford wouldn't notice, and if he did, that he wouldn't mind.

By the time Jack and Mr. Ford got home, Jack's parents were ready to drive back to Indian River for the night. We all chatted by the door for a few minutes and then said good-bye. As Jack's parents pulled out of the driveway, Mr. Ford said, "I'm coming down with a cold and want to get to bed as soon as possible, but I need to call Betty first. May I please use your telephone?"

"Of course," I said, pointing to the phone, disappointed we wouldn't be able to visit with him longer. I busied myself in the kitchen while he talked with Betty. As soon as he hung up, the congressman said good night and climbed the stairs to the loft.

Excited that a nationally prominent person was spending the night with us in our little house in Conway, I couldn't sleep. I worried about Mr. Ford, who coughed most of the night and was back and forth from the loft to the upstairs bathroom several times. To make matters worse, Bobby woke up crying, and I had to run upstairs to quiet him. I prayed Mr. Ford would not come out of his room as I was going in or out of Bobby's door, just steps away.

Next morning, Mr. Ford was up and showered by 4:45. I knew he had to be tired; I certainly was. I got up to make coffee and orange juice, and fixed a plate of powdered sugar donuts.

"Good morning," he said cheerfully but quietly as he came down the stairs, mindful that the boys were still sleeping. He set his small overnight bag and leather briefcase on the floor by the front door. His briefcase was well worn; obviously something he had carried for years. For all his political success and national prominence, Congressman Ford struck me as a humble man who couldn't care less about making an impression, caring more about connecting with people in a sincere and meaningful way.

Sitting down at the kitchen table, he said, "How nice of you to get up so early to fix my breakfast."

"Oh, I'm happy to do it. It's not much. I hope it's enough to keep you going until you get a decent meal."

"How did you know that juice, coffee, and a powdered sugar donut is my favorite breakfast?" he asked. "This is perfect."

While Jack got ready to leave for the airport, Mr. Ford and I chatted in the kitchen. He asked about the boys and talked about his own four children. He said being away from home some two hundred nights each year was the one thing he didn't like about the job he otherwise loved.

Well aware of Vice President Spiro Agnew's difficulties for alleged income tax evasion and President Nixon's mounting difficulties from the Watergate scandal, I boldly asked Mr. Ford, "Do you ever think about becoming president?"

"Others have mentioned that possibility, but I never give it any thought. I have more than enough to do to keep me busy."

A few moments later, Mr. Ford and Jack were out the door and into the chilly morning darkness. Jack carried the congressman's bag to the car as Mr. Ford turned to me. "Thank you for your wonderful hospitality," he said, taking my hand in both of his. "Bring those boys to Washington, D.C., but let me know ahead of time so I can arrange to meet you at my office when you come."

As he walked toward the camper, I called out to him, "We'll come to Washington when you become president, and you and Betty are in the White House." Grinning his wide, familiar grin, he waved once more, and they were off.

Several days later, a letter arrived from Mr. Ford thanking "the family" for the overnight accommodations. We also received a package from Washington containing a small pewter dish imprinted with the official seal of the U.S. House of Representatives.

On December 6, 1973, three months later, Congressman Ford became vice president of the United States. He was sworn in as president on August 9, 1974, by Chief Justice Warren Burger. In a televised address

The author's son, John Waldvogel, with a pewter bowl sent by House Minority Leader Gerald R. Ford after his overnight stay

from the White House East Room, he addressed the nation. "My fellow Americans, our long national nightmare is over. Our Constitution works; our great Republic is a government of laws and not of men. Here the people rule."

We were amazed that the same man who had slept at our little house in the woods just months earlier—a family man, a gentleman, and a man genuinely grateful for the simple breakfast I had served him at our kitchen table—was now president of the United States.

We never did go to Washington to see President and Mrs. Ford, but I did get to speak with former President Ford almost fifteen years later. I had moved to Grand Rapids and joined the Economics Club. President Ford was the honored guest at their first luncheon meeting of the 1988 season at the Amway Grand Plaza Hotel.

Just before dessert was served, I decided this was a rare opportunity I could not pass up. Aware that a Secret Service agent might intervene, I nonetheless left my place at the table and walked up to the head table. Nervous as I approached him, I relaxed when the former president smiled and held out his hand.

"Hello, Mr. President," I said, taking his hand. "In 1973, you stayed with us in our little house in the woods near Petoskey. You came up for a Republican Party fundraising dinner at Stafford's Bay View Inn. I just wanted to say hello."

President Ford looked puzzled for a brief second and then smiled. "Well, it's nice to see you again," he said graciously.

I knew he didn't remember me, but it didn't matter. I was thrilled to have spoken with him before and after he became president. Today, I am thrilled and grateful to be able to share this story with my grandchildren about the night we had a surprise overnight guest in our little house in the woods.

Leon H. Wilkinson, a retired farmer, engaged me to capture his life story as a legacy for his four sons, their children, and grandchildren. I conducted several interviews with Mr. Wilkinson at his retirement home. Based on those recorded meetings, I wrote his memoir, including the following story.

—Marjorie Keen

President Reagan's Visit

Leon H. Wilkinson, Narrator

In 1982, I was still working part-time as chairman of the Chester County Board of Assessment when I received a call from the Pennsylvania Department of Agriculture in Harrisburg. "Would you take two men from Washington around to show them some places they could bring U.S. Secretary of Agriculture John Block to discuss agriculture with the local farmers?" the caller asked.

I drove the men around Coatesville, Downingtown, and Elverson, Pennsylvania, on Monday to show them different farms that were well taken care of and were good family farms. My sons Charles and Tom were busy filling silos and felt it was more important to get their work done in time, so I didn't even take the visitors into our farm.

While we were driving along, I said, "Well, that farm up by Downingtown is really a nice farm."

One of the men said, "Yes, but I don't know about the security of the president."

"President?" I asked. "President who?"

"Well, if we can work the schedule that day, we may bring President Reagan along with us, too," he replied.

I realized then that things were getting more important than I had anticipated. When I dropped off the two men that afternoon, they told me that I would hear from them in a couple of days. Tuesday went by, and nothing happened. On Wednesday, I was at the Assessment Board when my wife, Edna, called. "Ten black cars just pulled in with a lot of black-suited gentlemen riding in each car," she said. "I think something important is going to happen at our farm."

By the time I got home, those gentlemen (Secret Service agents) wanted to know what kind of fuel was in the fuel tanks underground… What was in the silos? What was the ammoniated fertilizer stored in the shed? When they found out that the Delaware state line went across our pasture, they asked where the nearest police station was in Delaware and how many miles it was to the hospital. Everyone would have to be alerted in both states, they said.

My family and I decided we better get a shuffle and try to get ready for this important visit. Charles called the big aerial sprayer and asked when he could come down and spray-paint the barn. The painter told him ten days to two weeks, and Charles said, "I mean tomorrow."

"Well, I don't think I can do that," the man said. "How come it's so important?"

"I'm not supposed to tell you. But if you're going to help me, I'll have to tell you that the president of the United States is coming, and we need the old barn painted."

"I'll be there."

On Thursday, about a hundred of the farmers around and many of our neighbors, as well as some of the park workers sent by the county commissioners, came in to help us mow grass, paint the fence, and just tidy things up to get ready. About noontime, here came a big van with all the electronics so they could pull right in and start bouncing the pictures they wanted off the satellite. The telephone people asked me, "How many phone lines do you have in here?" I thought I was bragging when I told them two.

"That's not nearly enough. We'll have to have twenty-five or thirty to accommodate all the reporters."

One fellow with the Bell Telephone Company said he never saw a job processed so quickly. They got word at noontime and had a new cable line run into the farm by 2:30 p.m. to accommodate the situation. So a lot of things happened with the support of many people I didn't even know. By six or seven o'clock Thursday afternoon, it looked like we could accept the president the next day.

Charles Bakaly Jr., staff assistant and director of press advance for President Reagan, followed me around like a dog. I wondered what was going on and asked him, "Do you want to stay overnight with me rather than going to a motel?"

"That's the idea because I'm not allowed to let you out of my sight from now until the president comes and takes off again," he said.

After staying overnight at our rancher (a one-story

house), Mr. Bakaly only drank half a cup of black coffee the next morning. "Until the president gets on the ground and gets off again, I don't believe I want to eat," was his explanation. So you realize how much work goes behind a visit like this.

They had limed three circles for the helicopters to land in the cow pasture. When the first big chopper came in, television news anchor Sam Donaldson and all the reporters were on it. In the second chopper were senators and House members from Washington. Someone told me, "Now walk out in the middle of the cow pasture. The president will be arriving next." It was the most lonely feeling I ever had, standing out there alone in the middle of the cow pasture, waiting for a chopper to land in one of the big circles.

Before the president landed, the Secret Service agents had worked for several hours to get the 11,000-pound presidential limousine over the bank and out into the cow pasture. They had it all set up to show what the president was supposed to do. The little book said, "Leaving south lawn of the White House for Wilkinson farm." It had pictures of where we were supposed to walk and where we were supposed to stand, and it said the exact time we were to be at each designated spot. Finally, they had things all ready, and the president's chopper landed.

When President Reagan and Secretary of Agriculture John Block walked down the steps from the chopper, I welcomed them to Chester County. The president shook my hand. Then he took his coat off (it was a nice May day) and said that he was going to walk. That upset the Secret Service because a hike across the cow pasture wasn't in their plan.

President Ronald Reagan (left front) and Leon Wilkinson
(arm over rail fence) admiring Leon's herd, including
a new calf just christened Nancy No. 1

We walked up and hung ourselves on the rail fence to make it look real homey-like. This is where the christening of the baby calf took place. Sam Donaldson asked the president to milk a cow. But he was looking at a herd of expectant mothers (dry cows), so I told him it just wouldn't work. I christened a new calf Nancy No. 1 and talked shop with Reagan as we walked to the big hay shed, where the people were gathered. We sat on bales of straw and listened as the president made a short speech, fielded questions from the concerned farmers, and introduced members of his cabinet, senators, congressmen, and Governor Thornburgh of Pennsylvania.

Pictures of Ronald Reagan, John Block, and me were taken up at the hay barn. Then a lot of gentlemen who were running for election wanted to be in the act, too. After they finished taking pictures, the president and I were ushered over to the limousine. We drove down through a metal detector that everybody had to pass through. As we passed it, Reagan said to me, "The young farmers surely spoke from their hearts this morning."

"You better believe it," I said and shook my finger at him to make the point. We rode back across the cow pasture and out to the choppers. The president thanked me for the warm welcome and for our hospitality before he took off for a meeting in Philadelphia.

Someone took a picture through the limousine window of me shaking my finger at President Reagan that day. It has been kind of a joke ever since. They said that a farmer like me would be about the only one that could get away with something like that. The picture hangs in one of the halls down in Washington now.

An excerpt from a history I wrote of a fourth-generation family business, this is the story of how one man bought a small business three months before the Great Depression began and gradually, through hard work, gumption, and an innate business sense, grew it beyond expectations. David Potgeter and his successors cultivated a work ethic and sense of industry that is at the heart of their company's achievements today. In 2004, the Etna Supply Company, headquartered in Grand Rapids, Michigan, became one of the top fifty PVF and plumbing distributors in the United States, with three hundred employees at thirteen branches generating $150 million in sales.

—Debra Moore

The Legend of David Potgeter

Debra Moore

From all accounts, David Potgeter was a legendary man. Blessed with an outgoing personality, superior physical strength, a strong will, and a compassionate heart, Dave made a lasting impression on everyone he met. He has been described as honest, unique, talented, and inventive. Most of all, Dave had a tremendous work ethic that set the tone for his plumbing supply business, which would one day become Etna Supply Company.

Born in Allendale, Michigan, in January 1895 to Johan and Susanna (Mohr) Potgeter, Dave was the second of eleven children. The family, dedicated members of the conservative Christian Reformed Church, moved to Lynden, Washington, when Dave was three years old. Following a visit with relatives in Allendale in 1904, Dave's father became very sick at the Chicago Railroad Depot on their way back to Washington. The Potgeters returned to the Grand Rapids area to nurse Johan back to health. They never left.

Dave's formal schooling lasted through the eighth grade. A black-haired, brown-eyed youth, he worked throughout his adolescence on the family farm. He was a bright and knowledgeable young man, talented in many areas. Drafted during World War I, he was a bugler, played the piano, and sang. The war ended before he left the States, however, and the Army didn't provide him with a ticket home. Dave worked his way back to Grand Rapids with a friend, distracting farmers and killing their chickens to eat when necessary.

As a civilian, Dave got a job delivering coal for the Bennett Fuel Company. He wasn't happy when Bennett's laid him off despite his seniority and position as top-worker. "The other fellow has a wife and two children to support," he was told. "You don't."

Dave was forced to consider his options. He looked to purchase a coal company of his own. Warm Friend Coal Company, a business started a few years earlier by A. D. and H. M. Kaylor, was available. Dave bought the two men out on July 18, 1929.

Warm Friend was one of ninety-six Grand Rapids companies delivering coal, coke, and wood to homes and businesses. The company's office was located at 2691 South Division Avenue, next to the railroad tracks and just inside the budding suburb of Wyoming Township. Many of Dave's customers were the greenhouse owners along 32nd Street and environs. Naturally, business was good during cold weather. It also helped that growers used coal year-round to sterilize their dirt, and that residential customers with sufficient means filled their bins in the summer for the winter ahead. To fill the need, Dave engineered and built a 30-foot conveyor that was used for many years to move his coal from the railroad cars to the delivery trucks at Warm Friend. He was a natural, inventive handyman.

Dave employed an "office girl," Claire Wiersum, to answer the phone while he made deliveries and shoveled coal. As the business grew, he hired a few men to help him, but Dave always set the tone as the hardest worker.

Dave Potgeter with his "office girl," Claire Wiersum,
in the early days of the Warm Friend Coal Company

"He went home at night, filthy black with coal dust," remembered employee Ed Koster. "In the morning, he'd already shoveled a whole carload of coal before we saw him, so we never saw him clean. It was comical." This earned him the nickname Black Dave.

"Dad worked fifty-two weeks a year," said Dave's son Larry. "There was no such thing as 'vacation.' That was a dirty word, like 'laziness.' The first time he had to give the guys a vacation, he was madder than all get out. 'Here's your money!' he said as he threw it down on the table and growled, 'See you in three days.'"

In his prime, Dave was 5 feet 9 inches tall and weighed 180 pounds. A strong man, he could balance a 300-pound cast iron tub on his back and walk it up a stairway with a partner behind him for support and guidance. His hands were legendary. "He had hands like hams," said Leon Maack, another employee. "The first time I saw Dave, I noticed the size of his hands, but I thought it was due to an accident when one of his hands was broken. I found out Dave's hands were just naturally big through work. He had to use his pinky to dial the telephone; his other fingers were that thick." Those thick fingers also affected his piano playing.

Dave's heart was big in a quiet way. He extended credit to greenhouses that couldn't pay until they sold their crops. He filled family coal bins and waited for payment when their wages came in. Dave "never lost a penny" having faith in people—his trust was always rewarded. In addition, he loaned money to several friends and friends-of-friends to start businesses. If Dave trusted that you were "legit," few details were needed to secure a loan.

Shortly after buying Warm Friend, Dave married Louise Petersen in 1929. They had two sons. Roger was born on March 31, 1930, and Larry arrived on April 25, 1933.

Not a man for idleness, Dave lived with his family on a farm at 2121 32nd Street, on the north side of the street between Kalamazoo Avenue and Breton Road. He also had another farm about a mile away on Breton Road, halfway between 32nd and 44th streets. In the summertime when the coal business was down, Dave did the bulk of the farm work. He grew hay, corn, and oats, and tended cows, chickens, pigs, and a few turkeys. For a while, he used a horse for cultivating but eventually replaced it with a tractor. Dave's sons Roger and Larry used to drive about fifteen head of cattle down 32nd Street to the Breton Road farm to put them to pasture. One steer knew the way and, until his demise, led the group each time.

Larry recalled, "Dad would sit down after dinner, and that was it for the day. He worked so hard that he'd be asleep in bed by 8:00 or 8:30 p.m."

Dave never gave up the farm on Breton. As late as the mid-1970s, Larry's sons Mark and David helped out on the farm, picking corn and doing other chores. Their grandfather told the boys he'd pay them "farmer's wages," which meant room and board. It wasn't until he was seventy-eight years old that Dave referred to himself as retired.

When Ted Hull asked me to write a memoir of his years as the private tutor and road manager for the renowned, teenaged musical artist, Stevie Wonder, I gladly agreed. The Wonder Years: My Life and Times with Stevie Wonder, *the result of our collaboration, was published in 2000, and movie producers are beginning to express interest in the book. The following is a portion of the chapter titled "Be Cool, Be Calm."*

—Paula Stahel

Motown, Black and White

Ted Hull with Paula Stahel

Like me, most of the black people at Motown had their roots in the South. Several, such as Stevie's mom, Clarence Paul, Shorty Long, and Otis Williams, came to Detroit as young adults. Others, like Diana Ross, were born after their parents came north during World War II, often for factory jobs. But unlike my friends and colleagues, I was the minority at Motown—a white man born in Tennessee.

Northern whites, especially during the 1960s, tended to consider themselves "superior" to Southern whites on racial issues. But they weren't different in their prejudices, just in the way they expressed them. Too often, I recognized, Northerners respected blacks as a race but wanted nothing to do with them as individuals. In the South, it seemed the opposite. Some whites could care deeply about the black individuals who were part of their lives, yet remain staunchly opposed to racial equality.

Most of the Motown Revues played down South. It was where our strength was in record sales and recognition. And the tours were popular with many of the artists. I often heard, "Down South, I know where I stand. Up North here, they don't tell you."

All of us were young and naive enough to think things should be different. Only weeks before the second Motown Revue, President Lyndon Johnson had signed the Civil Rights Act of 1964 into law, "eliminating the last vestiges of discrimination," as the press reported. Things were supposed to be better for everyone. Besides, the Motown artists were famous stars, important in the music industry and to their fans. But what the law said and how whites felt were two very different things. If your skin was black, bigots didn't give a hoot if your name was Marvin Gaye, Diana Ross, or Stevie Wonder.

On the Revue in 1964, I quickly discovered how blatant discrimination could be. At a restaurant in Georgia, someone went inside to let them know we had a bus full of people hungry for lunch. Word came that everyone was welcome—around back in the kitchen. A joke was made that I could eat in the restaurant if I wanted.

Cynical humor covered much of our anger over such treatment, and my bus mates enjoyed seeing how I'd react to such first-hand treatment. I handled it like they did, accepting the fact that this was how it was, but not liking it one bit. We all walked around to the kitchen, got our lunches, and ate them on the bus.

Another time, just after passing a John Birch Society sign proclaiming "Martin Luther King is a Communist," we stopped at a restaurant crowded with lunch diners, only to see a white face hastily pull down the window shades and stick the "Closed" sign on the door. At times like that, it wasn't easy for me to remain philosophical or lighthearted with Stevie.

Stopping during the day might have been uncomfortable, but after dark, we knew things could get downright dangerous. On the 1963 Motown Revue, shots had been fired at the bus after the Birmingham, Alabama, show. It was bad enough for blacks, but adding my white face to the group only compounded problems. White Freedom Riders from the North were particularly reviled throughout the South, often beaten and occasionally murdered. In fact, shortly before the 1964 Motown Revue, three young Freedom Riders—two white men and a black man—disappeared in Mississippi. Our tour was long over before their bodies were found.

During the summer of 1966, Stevie and I drove part of the tour with his music director, Clarence Paul, instead of riding on the bus. Along with us was Joe Thomas, who was in his early twenties and working as Stevie's valet. Dusk was falling, and after a day on the road, we were hungry. On the outskirts of a small Georgia town, Clarence pulled his big black Chrysler into a drive-in. All the faces in the cars around us were white. I could feel the question hanging in the air: What were these three black guys up to, and how come a white guy was with them?

Racial tension was high all across the country. I was apprehensive, concerned about what these Georgians were thinking and what they might do. I reached for the set of bongos we had in the car and put them on the dashboard. I figured it was the quickest, most obvious way to settle any questions about who we were. Clarence understood, but Joe let out a hoot of derisive laughter. "Oooh, I think Teddy's scared."

Damned right! I thought, *Ted's real nervous because Ted wouldn't be the first white guy to take a bullet down South. And get his black friends killed along with him.*

But we tried to pull humor out of situations whenever we could. Finding public facilities was almost as much a problem as finding places to eat. On the way out of Atlanta after a gig at the Peacock Lounge, Stevie asked Clarence to find a restroom. Stopping at the next service station, Clarence said, "Come on, man, I'll take you."

Typical of the times, the gas station's bathrooms were segregated. Clarence steered Stevie through the "whites only" door and waited. As they walked back to the car, the attendant ran out the station door, sputtering in rage.

"Hey, man! Can't you see the sign? You can't ... You not supposed to take ... You're not supposed to use that bathroom!"

"I didn't." Clarence's voice was pleasant, and they kept moving. "He did. Besides, man, he's blind."

"Well, *you're* not blind," the attendant snapped.

Clarence opened the car door and Stevie got in. "Yeah, but, man, I didn't have to pee, either."

Segregated facilities presented a bit of a dilemma for me. Stevie and I were out for a walk one day in Tennessee when we decided to stop at a Dairy Queen. "You're not going to believe this," I told Stevie. "They still have separate windows for coloreds and whites."

"Which one are we going to?" Stevie asked.

"Since I'm paying, we both go to the whites,'" I said.

Finding decent food and lodging were our two most important concerns on the road. Motown always made our room reservations before we left Detroit. Often, though, the hotel management wouldn't know until we showed up that forty-nine out of the fifty of us were black. On more than one occasion, I went in first to let them know, make sure the reservations were in order, and just generally break the ice. I appreciated that whoever had first suggested it had confidence I had the right attitude to handle what could be a delicate situation. The concern was that if our entire group walked in together, we'd be told, "No, we don't have any reservations. You can't stay here."

Only once did a hotel owner try to turn us away, on a stop in Virginia. I immediately realized it had nothing to do with his personal prejudice and everything to do with fear. And I understood why. While we'd be leaving the next day, his livelihood could be seriously threatened by his neighbors and the community. We reached a compromise with the help of another hotel: our room reservations would be honored if we'd agree to eat at the hotel across the street. It was a way of sharing the responsibility and reducing local tension.

We agreed. We hadn't planned to eat at our hotel anyway. Most of the Motown musicians had played in these towns before. They knew where the black restaurants were, where we'd be accepted and could get good soul food. Those were the places we wanted to go.

Many a time, we'd arrive in a new city for a gig and have no idea where we'd be appearing. Especially in the early years, it was usually in the black part of town. We'd find the right area, stop somebody on the street and ask, "Where's the dance?" Everybody would know where the dance was being held, and that's where our show would be.

In those days, the Revues played some real bad places, often stark armories with terrible acoustics, in neighborhoods where white people were afraid to go, especially after dark. And more than once during a show, a gunshot or two would ring out. The band and all the artists would dive for backstage. Sometimes, after order was restored, the show would go on. Usually, though, it was two-thirds over by the time some guy got drunk enough to make a pass at someone else's girl. We'd just wait for the cops to arrive and clear out the crowd, then get back on the bus and take quiet leave.

Writing my mother's family history led me to cousins I had never known, like Maureen McKinzie Thomas. Still a beautiful woman at seventy-five, Maureen kept me spellbound with her stories about grandparents, parents, and siblings in early twentieth-century Texas. Both Maureen and her mother, Bess Dixon McKinzie, were famous for their cooking, so their recipes were a must in our family history cookbook. The following story is recorded in the archives of Abilene Christian University as Bess's Christmas Cake. But Maureen said, "They got it wrong. I was there!" When I told the university staff about Maureen's version, they bought a copy of our book, The Merry Campbells and Dixons (1998), to correct their records.

—Sharon Levine Waldman

The Cake That Saved a College

Maureen McKinzie Thomas, Narrator

My mother, Bess McKinzie, had a lot of recipes that she became quite famous for in Abilene. She was known for her Christmas pound cake, but it was her Fresh White Coconut Cake that saved the school.

In 1924, when I was fourteen months old, we moved from Hillsboro to Abilene because Dad had six children to educate and he wanted them to attend Abilene Christian College. It was just a tiny college in the middle of town then, with no place to grow. Dad had a ranch and dairy farm north of town, and he helped move the college near there. He worked as a fiscal agent for them but never took a salary. He did everything he did for his love of the school.

At one point in 1933, during the Depression, the college was thirty days away from bankruptcy because they couldn't pay back their loans. So Dad and another fiscal agent, Mr. Manley, traveled to Boston to meet the chairman of the bank that carried the papers on the school. The chairman was seated up on a kind of pedestal at a huge desk, and Dad and Mr. Manley were supposed to sit in two chairs below him. Instead, Dad picked up his chair, went around, and set it down by the chairman. He said, "I never could sell a fella on anything if I had to look up to him." Immediately, the man liked Dad.

"All I'm asking for is a thirty-day extension," Dad told him. "I have a wealthy oilman in Texas who I'm trying to get to donate the money we owe you. If you give us that extension, I might be able to do it in time."

"You've got it," the chairman said.

So Dad went back to a little town near Abilene called Burkburnett and called on John G. and Mary Hardin, a wealthy couple who had donated a million dollars to Simmons University, which had then changed its name to Hardin-Simmons University.

The Hardins lived on a farm. They had oil wealth, but they still used the old oilcloth tablecloth. After lunch or dinner, they would throw a white sheet over it, as the farmers did in those days. Dad had always been a farmer on the side, and he was a farmer at heart. So he and Mr. Hardin really got along well.

Mr. Hardin came to Abilene to see the college, and he was very impressed with the Christian education they were offering young people. Though Mr. Hardin was not a member of the Church of Christ, Dad knew that his first wife, Cordelia, who had died, had been a member. So he told Mr. Hardin, "Now, we will not name the college for you. It's called Abilene Christian; it will always be Abilene Christian."

Mr. Hardin said, "If you'd told me you were going to use my name, I wouldn't have given you any money. I'm really mad at Simmons for giving that college my name. I didn't want it."

Dad said, "But we would like to do something for you. Our administration building is being built. We're going to name it the Cordelia Hardin building after your late wife." That pleased Mr. Hardin.

Two weeks went by, and Mr. Hardin hadn't come through. Finally, Dad got him to come to Abilene one more time, and he decided to bring him to our house for four o'clock coffee.

Now, we always had four o'clock coffee at our home. It had been tea at Grandma and Grandpa Dixon's house years earlier, like their parents did in England. But with my mother and dad, it was coffee. Mother always had something baked fresh every day.

The men walked in, and Dad said, "Bess, this is Mr. Hardin. Do you have any coffee ready for us?"

"John, I just baked a fresh coconut cake. You all sit down, and I'll serve it."

They sat down and had cake and coffee. Mother's cake was beautiful—three layers piled high with white icing and fresh coconut. I know because I helped peel and grate the coconut.

Up until this time, Mr. Hardin had not given Dad a yes. But as he walked out the door, he patted Mother on the arm and said, "I'm glad to meet you, Mrs. McKinzie. It would be so hard now for me to deny your husband the money he's asking for, when his wife served me a piece of cake like that."

They named a dormitory at Abilene Christian College after Mother because she saved the college with her cake.

Maureen McKinzie Thomas, still baking delicious cakes

Bess's Fresh White Coconut Cake

This recipe makes three normal layers or four thin layers, like a tart. It serves from twelve to sixteen, depending on how you slice it.

    1/2 cup butter (1 stick)
    2 cups sugar
    3 cups flour
    3 teaspoons baking powder
    Pinch of salt
    1 cup milk
    1 teaspoon vanilla extract
    1 teaspoon lemon extract
    1 teaspoon orange extract
    8 egg whites, beaten until stiff (semi-hard, not dry)

Preheat oven to 350°.

Grease (or spray with nonstick spray) and flour cake pans. Cream the butter and sugar together. Combine flour, baking powder, and salt, then mix into batter alternately with milk and extracts. Fold beaten egg whites into batter.

Divide mixture between three 9-inch cake pans.

Bake for 20 to 25 minutes. Do not open oven for 20 minutes.

Maureen's Never-fail White Divinity frosting

Water for bottom of double boiler
1 cup sugar
1/4 teaspoon salt
1/2 teaspoon cream of tartar
2 egg whites
3 tablespoons water
1 teaspoon vanilla

Fill bottom pan of double boiler with water. Put all ingredients except vanilla in top pan of double boiler and begin heating.

When water in lower pan begins to boil, and a small white line begins to form from egg, immediately begin mixing with electric mixer while in pan. Beat for exactly 3 minutes, then remove from heat. Add vanilla and blend before frosting the cake. Frost between each layer, around the sides, and as a topping.

Grate 2 coconuts. Sprinkle fresh coconut on each layer and on the top.

Note: For Fresh White Coconut Cake, I would make the icing recipe twice, in order to have plenty of icing for the fresh coconut. Then grate 2 coconuts and sprinkle liberally on icing. —*Maureen*

A *few years ago*, a fellow personal historian
formed an Internet memoir-writing group with other
members of the Association of Personal Historians.
She assigned a monthly topic. Those of us who wanted
to would write a short memoir, which we submitted to
the group by e-mail. It was a wonderful way to experience memoir writing and get to know each other. As a
result, we gained a better understanding of how to help
our clients. The following is a story I wrote during
that group experience.

—Diane Dassow

One Small Step

Diane Dassow

I hear the small engines grind their way through today's latest snowfall.

I close my eyes and let my mind slip back to the sounds surrounding snowfalls from an earlier time—a time when we'd awaken to a smooth, brushing sound breaking through a perfect silence. It was the runners on the sled the boy towed along to deliver the morning newspaper. In nicer weather, he'd pull his Radio Flyer wagon, but its wheels would surely have gotten caught up in the white stuff. Later, shovels would scrape the sidewalks as dads or older brothers cleared the way for children to walk to school.

As thoughts of snowfalls turn to winter schooldays, a not-so-happy memory interrupts my reverie.

It was Chicago in 1954. I was in kindergarten. Sister Mary Hubert had devised a way to get all her fifty-plus charges suited up for dismissal on snowy days by assigning helpers. Those select few, as I recall, may have been students who'd already passed their fifth birthday. (As a November baby, I had entered school still several months shy of five.) The helpers had the task of assisting us less-mature students with our many layers of outerwear. Under our coats, many of us wore snow pants—bulky one-piece garments that buckled at the shoulders and snapped at the waist.

The day of the first big snowfall that winter, snapping and buckling were troublesome for my little fingers. Sister noticed my difficulty and dispatched a girl named Joan to my aid. I'm not sure why, but I balked and wouldn't let her help me. A warning from Sister didn't change my mind. I was told to take my things and go to the office.

I had never seen the office before. But to my kindergartener's eyes, it looked foreboding as I approached it that day. I began to cry as the principal escorted me behind the enormous front counter; I was instructed to sit there while my mother was called. All I can remember clearly is crying the whole time I waited for my mother to come. I think I was sitting on the floor, half-dressed in my snow pants and surrounded by my coat and other belongings, imagining the worst about what would happen to me.

My mother was probably beside herself, too, when she got the call. She had a baby at home, was pregnant, and did not drive. I don't recall how she got to school, but she must have called someone for a ride. We lived in my paternal grandmother's house, so Nonna probably watched my baby sister while Mom came to get me.

I don't think either parent yelled at me or punished me over the incident. But that evening after supper, Dad sat me down and instructed me on how to get into and out of my cold-weather clothes. We practiced over and over until I could manage the buckles and snaps alone. He had me pull my boots on and button up my coat, too.

Whenever a snowfall takes me back in thought to that winter day, I recall the feelings of smallness and helplessness as I sat in that scary school office in tears. I also feel the understanding of my parents.

Most of all, I feel the love and patience of my father, as he helped me take one small step toward confidence and independence.

Diane Dassow with her father, Archille Marchiori,
who guided her one small step at a time

In addition to encouraging others to preserve their
life stories, personal historians should set a good example by creating their own memoirs. I wrote this story
one month after finding my birth family. I was fifty-six
years old. At the time, I was a member of an APH
Memoirs Group, and this was my submission. I read
it at the closing session of an APH conference held in
Baltimore, an event by long-standing tradition called
Tales of the Heart.
—Libby J. Atwater

A Worthwhile Search

Libby J. Atwater

My hands shook as I touched the telephone keypad,
carefully inserting the ten digits that would connect
me with someone I had been waiting my entire life to meet:
my birth mother. Only one day earlier, on the ninety-eighth
anniversary of my adoptive mother's birth, I sent out six
identical e-mails before lunch:

*I am a personal historian seeking information on Angela
Scaglione, who lived in Irvington or Newark, New Jersey, in the
late 1940s. I found your name through the Google search engine
and thought you might help me with this project. If you have any
information that might help my search, please reply via e-mail or
telephone me at the number listed below.*
   Thank you, Libby Atwater

Within an hour, I received a reply:

I know this person. What kind of information are you look-
ing for? For whom and why?
Thanks, Jerry Scaglione

I wrote back immediately.

Thank you for responding to my query. The reason I am
seeking this information is for my own personal history. I was
born in Irvington General Hospital on February 15, 1948, and
my birth mother is listed as Angela Scaglione. I was given up for
adoption shortly after my birth, and I have always wondered
about my birth mother. My adoptive parents, Ruth and Harry
Kaplan of Hillside, New Jersey, died in 1962 and 1963, when I
was a teenager. I was afraid to seek my birth mother and family
for many years, unsure of what I would find. However, I would
really like to know my history for a number of reasons. I have
had some health problems that may have biological links, and I
have two grown sons who share my heredity. It would also be
very nice to meet my birth family if, and only if, they feel the
same way. I hope the information I have provided will not shock
or upset you. I would really appreciate your help.
Sincerely,
Libby Atwater

The reply came back within minutes.

Yes, it is a little shocking, and I am investigating this with a
few family members. I will get back to you ASAP.
Take care, Jerry

After this reply, I became nervous—afraid I would not hear from Jerry again—and volunteered some additional information. I heard nothing for the remainder of the day.

The next morning, I opened my e-mail immediately. A note from Jerry was waiting:

You are definitely a member of our family. The circumstances of your birth are a little different from what you were told—except for the Italian part. I am your first cousin. My father, your uncle, will talk to his sister today and ask her if she'd like to meet you. Please send me a phone number and the times you can be reached, and I'll call you later. Whether or not she wants to talk to you, you have a right to know.

I was so excited I felt I could fly, and no one was around to share my news. My husband was in business meetings all day, and my sons and daughter-in-law were at work. I couldn't leave the house, afraid I'd miss Jerry's call. It came at 5:30 p.m. "You have a mother, a brother, and a sister who all want to meet you," he announced. "Unfortunately, your father died in August 2003, but the rest of your family is alive and very happy that you found them. Here are their phone numbers."

Now I was dialing the phone. I listened as it began to ring—once, twice, a third time. Finally, a woman picked up. "Hello," she said.

"Is this Angela? I'm Libby, your daughter."

"How are you?" she asked, with a thick New York accent. "I always wondered what happened to you. It's been more than fifty-six years."

"I'm fine. I'm really fine, thank you. I've wondered about you all my life."

"Have you had a good life?"

"I have a very good life. There have been some ups and downs along the way, but I'm doing fine."

"I'm so sorry you didn't find me sooner," she said. "Your father would have loved to meet you. He died last year. I miss him terribly."

"I'm sorry I didn't get to meet him, too. What was he like?"

"Oh, he was such a happy guy. Loved music. From the moment he got up in the morning, that radio was on. Towards the end, he had problems—mini-strokes. He began to wander, and I had to lock him in the house when I went out."

Quite a while later, Angela said, "This call must be costing you a lot of money."

"It's all right. I've waited too many years to make it." Before hanging up, I told her, "Thank you."

"For what?"

"For giving me life," I answered and began to cry.

From our conversation I learned the parts of my story that I had been seeking for a long time.

My mother, Angela Brach, is now seventy-two; my brother John is fifty-five, and my sister Barbara is forty-nine. Robert Brach, my father, died in August 2003, shortly before his seventy-third birthday. He married my mother ten months after I was born, and they were together for more than fifty-five years. I have three nieces, three nephews, and a great-niece. They are a warm, loving Catholic family. The family believed in *omerta*, silence until death, and only my mother, father, aunt, and uncle knew of my existence until the day my e-mail arrived in my cousin's inbox.

My father's family was of German descent; my mother's, Italian. I was told that they fell in love quite young, although they had been forbidden to see each other. When my mother became pregnant with me

Libby and Angela celebrating their first Christmas together

at fifteen, she did not tell her parents. She was afraid that her father would kill her and the young man she was secretly seeing. On the day I was born, she didn't feel well and declined to accompany the family on an outing. Her father insisted that she go with them and was ready to strike her when my aunt interceded. "She's pregnant, and she's in labor. Don't you lay a hand on her! We're taking her to the hospital right now." With that announcement, Aunt Fran and Uncle Joe put my mother and their ten-month-old son, John, in the car and sped away.

I was born several hours later. My mother held me for a minute, and then a nurse came and whisked me away. "This baby is going to be adopted," she said. When my aunt and uncle asked if they could raise me, my grandfather was adamant. My birth would cause the family shame.

My grandfather had a reputation for being heavy-handed and controlling. But he could not control my mother, no matter how hard he tried. Later that year, she became pregnant with my brother John; my parents married seven months before his birth. Afterwards, they had three more children. A son was stillborn, and my sister Rosemary died from congenital heart disease when she was only thirteen months old. Barbara was born the following year.

Ironically, my birth family lives in New Jersey, only a few miles from where I was raised. We frequented some of the same stores and amusement areas but never met. I was startled to learn that I was the firstborn of five children. I've always had firstborn tendencies, although I was the younger child in my adopted family. After I heard my story, I joked that I was the first waffle—the one you throw away.

Reflections

Ruth Ann Newby, Narrator

*L*ife is what happens . . .

One of my favorite quotes is by John Lennon: "Life is what happens when you're making other plans." When my husband, David, was diagnosed with Alzheimer's disease, I thought about that quote often. I even tried the Scarlett O'Hara approach, "I won't think about that now; I'll worry about it tomorrow," but it was hard to maintain. Basically, I just hated being unhappy and worrying about things I couldn't change. You can't choose what happens to you, but you can choose how you react to what happens to you.

Ruth Ann Newby

For instance, you can choose whether you want to be miserable. I know some people who enjoy being miserable and want to share their misery with others. Not me. I just want to be happy. Perhaps I developed some of my resolve from having a step-mother who was so stern. I kept telling myself, I'm not going to let this get me down . . .

It also helps to find humor in the things that you can, which is just about every-thing, in my opinion, other than the direst tragedies.

Perspectives on my loss of sight ...

I'd like to describe some of my thoughts on being blind. One of the problems is trying to calculate just how blind I am. Saying I have some peripheral vision doesn't mean a whole lot to most folks. As an example, whenever a waiter tried to hand me a menu, I used to say, "I can't read." But that just implies illiteracy. Now I say, "I can't see well enough to read."

One of the greatest joys of my life was reading. Now that I can't read, I'm grateful for books and magazines on tape. If necessary, I can usually find someone to read to me. I used to be a compulsive newspaper reader, savoring it cover-to-cover, including even the dullest things. I'd love to be able to sit and drink coffee and read the Sunday paper, but I can't tell you how much time I save by not having a daily paper to read. Thank God for television so I can still get some news.

Some of the things that being blind is not: It isn't painful; it isn't fatal or even life threatening. It limits you in different ways. Probably the biggest disadvantage is not being able to see my children's and my grandchildren's faces. They are locked in memory so I can bring them up whenever I want to, especially when I hear their voices. Not being able to drive cuts down on a person's independence, but it also reduces your shopping, which I suppose is an advantage.

There are other advantages. I am not able to iron. I am not able to cook a complete dinner. Scrambled eggs pretty well covers it. I am not able to do much housework or to do office work like filing. These are all real advantages.

Maybe the one word that best describes being blind for me is it is so inconvenient.

Proudest accomplishments …

Without a doubt, my proudest accomplishments are having four wonderful children and five grandchildren who have turned out the way they have, and snagging David Newby. He thought that he chose *me*, but he just didn't know.

I'm proud of the people who call me a good and loyal friend and that they trust me enough to share their confidences, knowing that I won't give them too much advice on how to solve their problems.

I'm also proud that people believe I am someone who can bring humor to many situations. That's a gift I'm proud to possess.

What matters most ...

There's no question about that: What matters most is family. When I was going to college at National Park, I had a psychology professor named Mr. Montfort. After I wrote a paper that he really liked, he called me in for a conference and said, "Now, what do you plan to do when you finish college?"

I said, "Get married and have a family."

"What a waste," he replied. Boy, was he wrong! He didn't say what career he had in mind for me, but I'm surely glad I chose the one I did.

I remember telling my father at one time that I wanted to go to law school and be a lawyer like he was. His response was that he knew I could do the work, but he cautioned me that it would be difficult for a woman. Had I chosen that path, I would have missed a lot. I was intent on marrying David Newby and having children, and I certainly succeeded at fulfilling both those dreams.

My country matters to me, too. As I write this, we are very involved in a war in Iraq, which I think we went into for false reasons, and I hate that.

If you'd only listen ...

I'm sure there were times I said to my own husband, "David, if you had only listened to me," but he certainly turned out very well. At this point in my life, I do have a few suggestions <u>if you'd only listen:</u>

Travel. It expands your horizons.

Save your money, but don't be miserly about it. Save enough to have a secure future, but always use it to help others.

Take care of your health.

Seek out and nurture meaningful, loving relationships.

You are blessed with fortune and health and so have an obligation to help *those who are not so blessed.* The joy in having money is seeing what good you can do with it.

Find a good, reliable financial adviser and invest as much as you can.

Try to *stay away from debt* as much as you can, but if you must go into debt, pay on the principal every chance you get.

Hopes for the future...

Looking back, I think it's a miracle that I have lived to be this old. Having done that, it's amazing that I've managed to stay this healthy and ended up as fortunate as I have. If you can say near the end of your life that you think that the world—or at least your part of it—is a little better off for you having lived, I believe that you could be happy with that. I think I've achieved that.

And finally, to my children and grandchildren: My enduring wish is that you stay close to each other all your lives and remain a family united in love. Always be there for each other. The love you give will be returned to you many times over.

My interest in personal history was ignited by the Foxfire books, first published in 1966. After a New York publisher heard about a project in Northeast Georgia, where high school students were interviewing some of the "local old-timers" in their community, those interviews were compiled into a book titled Foxfire. I eagerly devoured that book and each one in the series that followed. Years later, I met Willard Watson, whose 1975 interview was published in Foxfire 6. "I 'spect I better update that old story," he said, and with that he became the first non-relative to tell me his life story. Our interview took place in 1990 when Willard was eighty-five years old.

—Andrea Gross

Doin' Things One Way, The Right Way

Willard Watson, Narrator

"If I had a nickel for every time some'un pointed a camera at me, I'd be a rich man," says Willard Watson, giving me a crooked smile. He's right. Watson is a casting director's Mountain Man, complete with drooping mustache and the requisite attire—red and black flannel shirt, bib overalls, and broad-brimmed brown hat. Even the setting, a weathered wood shack surrounded by tall hemlocks and pines, is movie-set perfect. The October weather is brisk, and inside his workshop, a wood-burning stove chases away the chill.

While my husband snaps a picture, Watson holds a pose and then continues carving one of the toys that have made him famous. "People tell me they get lost finding this place," he says, "but I tell them, 'You ain't lost. You just where you ain't never been before.'" He pauses and looks at us quizzically. "You folks get lost?"

We tell him we had. Watson lives in Deep Gap, North Carolina, an aptly named settlement about two hours north of Asheville. When we called him the day before our visit, he'd given us directions: "You just come up the mountain a bit, and then when the hardtop ends, you turn left and go back down. We're here in the hollers."

We had to stop three times and ask for help, but people in these parts are used to pointing people toward the Watson place. "We get folks here from all over the world," says Willard. "A few years back, we had folks right square out of France. But the furtherest away anybody ever came was from Australia. Now that was a long way from their bed!"

He stops carving, leans back, and folds his gnarled hands in his lap. A satisfied smile creases his face as he tells us about his most famous visitor. "Charles Kuralt came and visited the other day. Sat right there at that table up in the house. He liked my toys.

"See, this here's a dancing doll. These dancing dolls were around when I was a boy, but most of the other things I make ain't never been seen before. Mostly, I jest make things that are in my head."

Watson's head is full of farmers chasing pigs to market, chickens scratching for corn, and horses pulling wagons or sleighs. His carvings, which have doubled in value over the last five years, are made out of whatever wood is available. He prefers lind and buckeye, but he tells us, "White pine's good, too, if it's been air-dried. Kiln-dried wood cracks."

In his conversation as well as his art, Watson dwells on the past, calling up vivid images of Depression-era Appalachia. He picks up a drill and continues working on an almost finished carving of a man driving a mule, prodding the animal along with a whip. Watson's devised a simple crank mechanism that allows the jointed figures to move. He keeps up a steady stream of talk as he carefully adjusts the crank to reduce friction.

This toy here is a handful of trouble, but there's just one way to do things, and that's the right way. I learned that early on. I've only been making toys since I started getting Social Security. I've made a lot of toys, but I ain't never kept count of just how many.

Nobody taught me how to carve. But if you get anything in your head or mind that you want to do, you just do it. One day I seen a mule and driver in my head, so I turned them out with my knife. Then I wanted them to move, so I made them do that. You got to use your head for something.

I guess I done just about everything since I was hatched. I didn't stay around home long 'cause there was too many things I wanted to do. I left with my cousin when I was fourteen. We went to this camp, and we didn't know nobody. I slept a night, and then I went to talk to the boss.

He said, "What can you do?"

And I said, "I'll try anything you got."

I was little, but I was tough, and I was made outa good stuff. So he hired me to hold the angle irons and the railroad spikes for the men who were driving the spikes. That was my job.

Then one day the boss left camp, and I picked up his spike-driving hammer. When he came back, I was a-driving railroad spikes, but I laid down the hammer when I saw him and went back to carrying things. Two, three days later, he got gone again. And when he got back, I was driving spikes again. "Watson," he says, "I see right now there's no keeping that spike-driving down. You just drive all the spikes you want to drive." So I did.

After that, I learned other things, too. I've felled timber, and I've ditched and worked at rock crushers and worked in coalmines. I've been under the ground three and a half miles from daylight. I pulled a crosscut saw hundreds of days for two dollars a day. There's nothing harder on a man's body than a crosscut saw and a jackhammer. I've made moonshine, too. There's a still out there in those woods.

So you can see I've been lots of places and had lots of good times. But I like what I do now the best.

Willard Watson carving wooden toys
"the right way" in a small cabin
in Southern Appalachia

Willard stands up and stretches. He's almost 6 feet tall, and he has to stoop to get through the doorway of his workshop. "We'll go up to the house and meet the old hen," he says in a gravelly voice. "She and me, we've been tied together sixty-four years now. She's the world's best biscuit maker, and she suits me just fine."

We walk about 100 yards to the house that, Willard tells us, he built himself "one room at a time." It's a compact one-story, wood-framed home with three bedrooms and a living room/kitchen centered around an old stone fireplace.

He introduces us to Ora, a short, sturdy woman with white hair tied back in a knot. She looks as if nothing fazes her. Not six children, thirty-four grandchildren, great-grandchildren, and great-great-grandchildren, and certainly not a husband who calls her an "old hen." She's an accomplished quilter. At our request, she shows us some of her quilts—a log cabin design in pastels for a double bed, a Texas lone star pattern in brown and white for a king size.

Ora points to the quilting frame hanging from the ceiling. "I just let it down when I'm working and pull it up when I'm finished. It works fine that way. It takes me a week to make a quilt if I piece steady, two or three days longer for a king size. Lots of people comes from Florida and wants them.

"I take care of the money they give me and the money they give Willard for his toys. You know, he cain't read. When he was young, he lived way down there in the hollers, and buses couldn't come get him to the school. He only went through third grade, but I finished seventh grade. Our children didn't go to no high school, but our grandchildren, they all graduated." She gives a satisfied nod. "That's good."

Willard walks back into the room, carrying a doll's bed covered with a hand-pieced quilt. "I made the bed for one of the young'uns, and she..." He nods at Ora. "She made the topping."

He sits down in a chair and runs his hand over the carved design on the small bed. "Some folks tell me I'm the best toymaker anywhere. I don't know as I'm the best, but my head and mind is happy doing this. And the things I make now are gonna linger on after me."

He looks at us with a satisfied smile. "Now my words are gonna linger on, too."

Index
Anne Burton Washburn